Travels on the Edge:

One Woman's Journeys
on a Runaway Planet

Travels on the Edge:

One Woman's Journeys on a Runaway Planet

MJ PRAMIK

Eight Palms Press

Photos:
All photos are by the author, except as otherwise noted:
Cover: Parahawking in Nepal above the Annapurnas
         (Location: Sarangkot Mountain, Pokhara, Nepal).
Page 6 Canal du Midi © André Cros / CC-BY-SA 4.0

Cover/interior design: Book Alchemist (www.bookalchemist.net)

CATALOGING IN PUBLICATION DATA:
Travels on the Edge:
One Woman's Journeys on a Runaway Planet
By Mary Jean Pramik

Published by Eight Palms Press

ISBN: 978-1-7331819-7-6

To my parents, Mary and Joseph, who started me on this journey, and to Danika, Madeleine, and Joe, who accompany me every step of the way. To all who have shared with me minutes of their life on this planet, may we continue to walk together.

Abandoned British base at Port Lockroy, now renovated into a museum on Wiencke Island, Palmer Archipelago, Antarctica.

Contents

CONTENTS

Glaciers climbing into the clouds cast a peaceful world about all who encounter them.

Preface

Our prime purpose in this life is to help others.

—Dalai Lama

Travels on the Edge challenges readers and travelers to wake up! wake up! wake up! to the wonders of this planet as it experiences unprecedented changes in climate and weather at warp speed. Just as the COVID pandemic raised the specter of mortality around every corner, the real promise of future pandemics, a rapidly warming planet, and extreme variations in weather will significantly affect travel plans. However, a glorious joy wells up in us when we visit a new part of the world. Many travelers would leave home even if assured that calamitous global fluctuations await them.

During the current time of one catastrophe after another—California, Australia, and Cuba burning, Antarctica and Greenland melting faster than predicted, India and Bangladesh swamped by heat waves and floods—everywhere we journey on this planet seems to place us face to face with unprecedented events. On a recent trip to the Middle East, I traveled two days ahead of Palestinian and Israeli hostilities, missed the

1

Turkey/Syria 7.6 magnitude earthquake by a day, and had to hole up in Cairo for an unplanned three-day interlude because of high winds and storms on the Mediterranean Sea that prevented our small ship from entering the Suez Canal.

When Shaman Juan Chiyal told me in the essay *Mayan Shaman: Your Life Will Change*, I'm sure he wasn't predicting the current climate catastrophe. But travel has changed me. This collection of travel stories offers my reflections on how the climate crisis may affect our attention to the habitats and people in each unique location that we visit. As the globe burns, melts, erupts, and floods, I feel an evolution of hope though. Scientists, environmentalists, governments, communities, and individuals are joining together to consider large and small solutions to the disruptions we now witness. I offer a Recommended Reading list to buoy your hope as well.

Raised as a lover of the natural world in rural Ohio, I trained as a biologist, have worked as a citizen scientist (as in the essay *Mongolian Disco*), and keenly understand how the climate crisis shapes our lives. I've traversed six of the seven continents and believe that travelers' tales can inspire joy in living with each other, and in solving problems together. My hope is that these stories may inspire you to wake every day to meet the challenges that we humans, nonhuman animals, and plants currently face.

After decades of crisscrossing the globe, I found

that the planet heals wounds, expands awareness, forges friendships, and engenders a faith about the future of life on earth. Together we can review human behavior and assess how we can help the planet heal. The COVID pandemic has underscored that we share the planet with more than eight billion humans and multibillions of nonhuman creatures and plants.

The essays and stories in this book, written over many years, are a collection of observations of my pilgrimages across the earth as I journeyed to visit or revisit places where climate issues now impact the places and the people I fell in love with. After each of these reflections, I offer a poem of hope for the future for I believe the poetry blesses us all.

The planet has a resiliency that will prevail after humans are gone. *In Ways of Being*, James Bridle tells of how animals, trees, and even slime molds communicate with each other and with other species. Travel experts have come to recommend slow travel. Rather than see and do and taste everything in a locale, why not go for quality rather than quantity. They suggest immersing oneself in the local culture, reaching deeper for a longer time. Some recommend shortening or even tearing up the to-do list. I've come to agree with many of these ideas. Gone from my recent trips is the blur of nonstop activity—climbing cathedral steps followed by museums, shopping, and restaurants all in a single day.

The travel industry generates eight to ten percent of global CO_2 emissions according to the World Travel

& Tourism Council. This Council, composed of travel industry representatives, local cities and destinations, governments, airlines, and hotels, has noted that flying creates the greatest amount of CO_2 in the atmosphere among all travel activities. Some countries have banned short flights if other modes of transport are available.

I've outlined for myself a Traveler's Code of Conduct as so many others have done during the shutdowns. My travel code's main points include travel purposefully, travel emphatically, travel slowly, and travel joyfully. All with the resolve to tread lightly on the earth as we meet others who share our lives.

When a person is faced with seeing the world or taking the responsible climate action of staying home, the trip usually wins. We know travel can be a burden on the planet. But many claim travel can be somewhat sustainable. If we lean in together and create solutions to lower our overall carbon footprint, we can continue to enjoy visiting the earth's awe-inspiring wonders and communicating with the peoples, nonhuman animals, plants, that rock this world.

Safe travels.

A stroll along the banks of the Canal du Midi can revive
anyone's belief in the planet's resilience.

Marie Jeanne:
Une Seconde Vie

France

For many years, my daydream was to board any flight to any destination, preferably international, and not inform anyone of my whereabouts. After twenty-five years, my marriage finally ended, and my children moved on to establish their own lives. I began to search for something to do for the rest of my life, something to fill the fast-approaching void. With one child a professional dancer in Pennsylvania, the second a recent college graduate sorting out life in Maine, and the youngest to start college, I knew I would soon have my chance to travel, to explore the world I had been missing.

Thus, on a desperate whim and a bit ahead of schedule, I signed onto a boat voyage on France's Canal du Midi, promoted as a writing conference. An attractive quality of the trip was the peaceable demeanor of the ship's captain. Knowing nothing about her, the boat, or the canal except that all three existed, I conducted a brief telephone interview and learned the basics. She had sailed solo across the Pacific the previous year, had two daughters in their twenties, was married to an attorney, loved boats, owned this one (named *Lurley*), and published books. I sent in my down payment the next day, an extravagant expenditure for me at the time.

I looked to this trip with a small boatful of writers as a safe space for travel without the plastic feel of a tour. It would add to and encourage my solo movement through the world—an experiment in putting myself out there, validating my existence. The writing conference would expand my work as a science writer. More rationalizations followed each week as the day of departure loomed.

It began in Paris. Our writing instructor, Linda, suggested viewing an exhibit of the later works of Matisse at the museum in the Luxembourg Garden. I knew Matisse well. I had always enjoyed his childlike forms and color cutouts that seemed so much like my children's drawings and paintings. More than a decade earlier, I had visited the Musée Matisse de Nice, which overlooks the city's amble along the Mediterranean. With children in tow, I had also made the pilgrimage to a church in Vence embellished by the artist's stained-glass windows that soared upward in search of light. Yes, I knew Matisse, which may have accounted for my indifference as I approached the exhibit.

Then the Greek crewmember, Connie, handed me an audio tour guide. I usually avoid such recorded lectures because I prefer to experience exhibits without being told what to see or feel. I favor experiential viewing. But I was in France, a new environment, so this time I listened. A descriptive recitation accompanied each section of the exhibit. I became entranced by the soothing male voice. The recorded host told of how Matisse had survived cancer after major surgery in 1941. Out of this painful time, the artist—now nearly eighty—became inspired and extraordinarily productive. He called these years his second chance at life, his "*seconde vie*." He had been given an opportunity to further develop and define his art. He moved into this task with fervor.

The 21 Trees, a series of twenty-one pen and ink drawings of mostly plane trees—stalwarts that line the Canal du Midi—led Matisse to describe the "birth of a tree in the head of the artist" in an intense twelve-year correspondence with his close friend, André Rouveyre. Each tree in pen and ink on paper began with a strong trunk, with Matisse drawing each leaf individually with reverence.

Then my favorite collection appeared: *Jazz*. This group of vibrant paper cutouts took on a deeper meaning now that my youngest offspring had decided to become a jazz musician, honing his abilities on drums, marimba, vibes, and piano. He repeatedly surprised me on our driving trips with his latest collections of jazz classics. "Mom's Birthday Mix" opened my ears to new colors of percussion and sound. I could hear him accompany Matisse's fourteen works in this suite.

Further into the winding galleries, I realized that much of Matisse's attraction grew from the simplicity of his cutouts—how the colors and shapes intertwine and cannot be separated. They express the same spirituality that shines through in the Amish quilts I grew up with in eastern Ohio. He cut colored paper and layered restless figures on pages, moving sheets here and there. Much like working on a jigsaw puzzle, if one squints and breathes slowly, the pieces place themselves. Matisse took this technique further. He left spaces between his cutouts where a thought or a person could find further definition.

Matisse confided to his friend Rouveyre that this second chance at life upon being cured of cancer, this *seconde vie*, had revealed to him the "space between things."

Hearing these words, I stopped mid-exhibit. The space between things. This was why I had come to Paris, to France, this year and this month, with these people. I had arrived here to try to become comfortable with the space that had developed around myself after half a century of living, to a place where I might reclaim my art and what remained of my life.

Then I saw *Zulma*. Rouveyre loved this painting, describing *Zulma* as the epitome of a woman. Matisse completed *Zulma* in 1950 when I was two years old. He cut and patched together a seven-foot-tall woman with an ocher core in her torso and black hair, cerulean blue arms and outer legs—not anatomically correct, but psychologically precise and insightful. *Zulma*—so many pieces and stresses pull at this woman. A cutout, she is inorganic, just pieces of paper. But she is human, glued together and holding on.

The cutout masterpiece from Matisse followed me to Toulouse after a five-hour ride on a high-speed train. The Toulouse sky radiated blue hues. The rose-colored bricks heated the outlines of the canal in the torpid afternoon.

"Let's walk," someone suggested. On a cool morning in Paris, the one-mile trek from the train station to the marina would have been wonderful. However, my thirty-seven-pound rolling suitcase full of books squashed any fun out of walking more than two blocks. I pulled, twisted, and sweated, all while muttering, "Next time, a taxi." We passed *La Purgatoire* bar along the Canal, the neon sign apropos of our prickly condition as we navigated uneven cobblestones and gray gravel.

I could not request help. All the others in the troop laughed and joked, not noticing my discomfort. We approached the marina and spied *Lurley*. Our *capitaine*, Barbara, waved a hurrah. One last pedestrian bridge, a mélange of irregular concrete stairs, was the ultimate challenge. My companions were far ahead. I was the shortest and the oldest. I felt like Joan of Arc, a martyr with a purpose. "*Jeanne d'Arc, c'est moi*" became my mantra with each struggling step.

Voila! Captain Barbara appeared with her gentle smile. Her welcome hug lightened my load immediately.

Once on board, a survival war began in earnest. Only three berths looked at all comfortable. I went to fetch my bags and returned to find all berths taken. The two quiet crewmembers, April and I, were allotted the smallest and most difficult-to-ascend berths. Difficult for short individuals, in particular, and nary a ladder in sight. A new lesson for the seconde vie: selfishness might be a required survival skill. *Jeanne d'Arc* the Second accepted the berth "under the torpedo," as my ex-husband used to describe his bunk on a Navy submarine. Neither April nor I had room to unpack our suitcases. But at least there were two toilets on board. It could have been worse.

The next morning, while others headed straight to the Sunday market, I searched the streets of Toulouse for an internet café to check emails. Refreshingly, none were open, hastening my separation from my "first life" of family, work, and worry.

We said *au revoir* to Toulouse on board our larger boat *Royal Destiny* that Sunday afternoon. We were seven sisters, the Pleiades. This plot might work, I thought: Seven would-be artists transition the locks to unleash their perimenopausal energy to the universe. Bicyclists and inline skaters escorted us out of La Ville

Rose, the Pink City. We waved and smiled.

A plane passed overhead while a luminous dragon-fly hovered and zipped around us close above the deck. Screaming locusts seemed to echo one another in a steady crescendo. Tensions on the boat reflected the thunder rumbling through the atmosphere. We were on a boat with nowhere to turn except to each other. We had ten kilometers to go before reaching the first lock. My jet lag kicked in after a lunch of country bread, morbier cheese laced with ash, and the obligatory wine-with-every-meal, this one a Chardonnay pleasingly named "Sainte-Marie de Pins." A smiling woman played her red accordion on a neighboring boat, lulling me into an afternoon stupor.

We tied up before the lock and awaited the arrival of Cristophe, a Sunshine Cruise Lines agent. He was to instruct the crew on how to navigate the locks. I did not recall reading this section of the trip planner; I didn't have a clue that I would be part of the crew and that we neophytes were to handle the ropes, or lines, as we were taught to call them. Judging by the calm blank looks on the faces of my travel mates, neither did they. We all were slowly coming to realize that not only were we attending a writing conference on a thirty-five-foot cruiser, but we were also the crew.

Cristophe knew only one speed—the stride. He strutted straightaway toward the moored vessel. His teaching technique reflected his gait. He propelled staccato instructions at the seven rapt women about how to hang the lines (black ropes) on the side of the boat so as not to pull the railing off when negotiating the locks, how to cast off gracefully and tie up securely with fanciful knots, and how to behave in the olive-shaped locks. He demonstrated how to prepare the ropes to toss them up to a crew member who has jumped off to warn (actually alert) the lock keeper that we wished to (phonetically) "sweat passé" (*souhaite passer*).

Passing through the first lock resembled a Keystone Cops comedy. Lesson One: Tossing lines *up* is more difficult than tossing them *down*. Our *capitaine* frowned on our lack of expertise.

"I'll get it!" one crewmember shouted.

"No! Toss it here. I'll do it," another offered.

"Wrap it quick around the bollard [a mushroom-shaped piece of metal bolted onto the ledge of the lock and ready to hold the line, a.k.a. the black rope]," the voice of the captain boomed.

"Oops," someone whispered.

"Here, try it again. Ready, aim, uh. Oops."

"Hey, I've got it! Ah, missed."

My melatonin had not kicked in, while the midday wine had. The frenzied scene said to my reptilian brain, *It will be better in the morning, or at least after a nap.* In the confusion, I pulled myself up into my uncomfortable bunk and fell asleep. I dreamed that I slept through a silent flotation of the Ark, with stupendous bumping and banging and shouting. The captain's seat vibrated hysterically. Fumes and fumes, two by two.

It seemed everything I did was wrong. Crew members grumbled that I had disappeared while *they* labored through the second lock without noticing that they had hijacked every job on board, leaving me to feel, well, slightly superfluous and insignificant.

Lightning in the east sliced the early evening sky. Thunder punctuated the tensions after a very long first day navigating the canal. Rain tapped into our respite as we huddled below in the evening, tied up at Montgiscard. The workshop leader lectured us about travel writing trends, writing about place, and the third-person omniscient narrator. I realized that I was very hungry irrespective of the time zone.

"Find your niche," said the instructor, and my mind flew to the isosceles triangle that was to be my sleeping quarters for the next six nights. Covered with a rather warm and fuzzy, ocher-colored blanket atop a two-inch-thick, plastic-covered mattress, the best term to describe my feelings was chagrin. At least the small porthole opened above the waterline.

After class, we had an intense group discussion about dinner. The sky had cleared, and we gathered on the upper deck. We could walk a mile into the nearest town to a restaurant, or we could cross the street and bring home pizza and salad.

I watched the swallows' aerial ballet, diving to the water's surface, darting close, then ricocheting apart back to the twilight sky. On the canal's surface, water striders skimmed along with their six legs akimbo. Some straddled their paramours from behind for a night of French love. Nearby, a Labrador retriever rustled his chains and lumbered into the shade of a doghouse flanked by a picket fence and red geraniums.

The vote was unanimous. The path of least resistance was *La Pizzeria de l'Écluse*, across the country road from our mooring. Excellent pizza and rosé, a Château Trois Moineaux de Gaillac. We sat atop the boat in the fading sunlight, enjoying the warmth of the oncoming evening.

At 3:43 a.m., all was quiet outside. A cat guarded the stone fence that bordered the opening to the lock. A red-and-pink neon circle spun a bleep-bleep-bleep continuously above the door of a video rental shop. Lightning jabbed the northeast horizon, and the cat disappeared along the stone fence into the darkness. I returned to my bunk from the prow of the cruiser. Everyone slept.

I began our second day by running alone on the tar path adjoining the canal. Gaining strength by finding my body moving through a familiar action, I decided to volunteer for tasks on the boat. I asked to take the helm. Under the watchful eye of the captain, I began steering wild S's, first left then right. After three hours of intermittent practice and centering my focus, the wheel felt solid, and my steering calmed. We had to duck under several low bridges before the captain took us through the deep double lock. Joel the lock keeper turned the water on full-bore to speed the filling. The boat bobbed with the turbulence, and the rope lines demanded enormous strength. I planted my sandaled feet solidly against the railing to keep from flying over the metal balustrade.

The Pleiades were indeed stars, all lighting up their distinct personalities once on the stage of the boat. I was still sorting out my melatonin and basal cortisol levels. My body normally requires five days to gain sea and land legs after crossing the Atlantic. With this group, I did not have the luxury of time; it was survival or else.

At times, our personal interactions grated and chafed against each other. "Be gracious," commanded one mate, handing me a bottle of water. "Don't take it personally," said another, not explaining how to take a critical comment impersonally. Joyce Carol Oates' and Alice Walker's zeal for solitude seemed most attractive at such moments. I found it difficult to write with all the laughter, singing, chatter, grandstanding, and intermingling. The boat's buzz flooded the pathways to what I thought and felt and drowned the space between the things I sought.

I tried to apply some of the instructor's *bon mots* about writing to living on the boat. "Don't strive to blend in, and don't retreat. Don't be shy about how you feel; this is what it's all about." And then, "Don't be fearful; use humor. You can relax and laugh. Stress, release."

We passed the peak of the canal, le Seuil de Naurouze, where the water begins to flow toward the Mediterranean. We tied up at Le Ségala, a small town surrounded by red clay tiles piled high at a tile factory.

The tile factory dominated the town. Walking through all four square blocks of the village, I began to gain a clearer understanding of what Matisse described as the space between things, space that sometimes binds people and places together.

We had a jovial supper at Le Relais de Riquet alongside the canal. "Josisanne pas [not] Josephine," laughed our hostess. Marquise, the resident canine, welcomed the Seven Maidens of the Midi, as we began to call ourselves. We shared a *cassoulet glacé* dessert made of ice cream, chocolate, and sweet sauce after our various main courses. With enough *vin du pays d'Oc*, each of us relaxed into our own spaces.

Our late-morning push-off allowed me to try one of the bikes. I needed to move faster than the boat's eight knots. The bike looked too large, but it fit me well enough. Pedaling past fields full of sunflowers again added new space to my trip. Through locks and more locks, I became expert at handling the lines around the bollards on shore.

In Castelnaudary, I found the center, that space around myself, like Matisse's red-and-black seaweed and azure balls of twine. I could look at the crew with open eyes and still hold onto who I was. This sense of presence allowed me to defend my actions with unquestioning zeal. Pushing back against the star-like Pleiades was slow in coming—goodness, a whole five days. Listening to the conversation, it did not matter that I had no famous friends or PhDs or extraordinary adventures. Why, I was just starting my seconde vie. Enjoying each of these six individuals for who they were ironically strengthened my sense of who I was. I laughed as I watched two crewmembers share an iPod programmed with Sixties favorites, dancing all the way back to the *Royal Destiny*.

It was time for the return trip. We aimed to reach Toulouse in about one-third the time it took to dock at Castelnaudary. Retracing our kilometers, it was difficult to steer into the headwind. I found the boat did not respond as before as the zigzagging wide S's returned. The *capitaine's* vibes said, *Please shape up*. My new sense of space said, *Hey, I can only do what I can right now*. We passed wildflowers that mimed the Queen Anne's lace of my childhood in Ohio. The roots of the plane trees lining either side of the canal resembled the claws of ancient birds holding the shores together. Duck families hid among the talons. Green leafy vegetation bowed overhead.

Later that day, I rode the bike for nearly twenty kilometers along the path. The surge of power on the old bike felt tremendous. I was the messenger to the lock keeper at Negra *écluse*, where we would dock for the night. As I staked out a docking site, Jean the lock keeper, with his wry smile and twinkling eyes, walked over to where I rested against the bike. We chatted in his excellent English and my half-French. He had served as a lock keeper for five years. He cared for the gardens around the lock and the chapel with its beautiful wood carvings as well.

Did he like this job? I loved the way the French say "pfoot" and roll their lips to answer such questions. Further explanations would have to wait as the *Royal Destiny* rounded the bend with our stalwart *capitaine* at its helm. I felt so present in that moment; only the word "joy" could describe my sense of place and space.

In the early morning, Linda and I ran past the fields of sunflowers with freeway noise rising in the distance. As we cast off from Negra, lock keeper Jean, with his wide grin and an enchanting scar on his left cheek, quickly picked a bouquet of his cultivated lavender and handed it to me as the boat sunk into the lock. Later I divided the stems among my fellow travelers to press in the pages of our writing notebooks.

In six days, traveling from Toulouse to Castelnaudary and back interrupted the frenzy of my American way of life. I focused on the moment. The locks served as newfound relationships, up and down, growing as long as we worked together navigating the Canal du Midi. We toasted each other as we neared our destination: "May the Pleiades, the Seven Sisters, shine on the Canal du Midi."

Rather than outlining a new life path or acquiring another personality during this maiden voyage on the Canal du Midi, I found instead the space between things, where I firmly resided. And that was enough.

FACT: The 2022 summer of storms, wildfires, and flooding that plagued Paris and pushed the Seine to overflow its banks, have now locked the Canal du Midi in a drought. Where and when my boat, the *Royal Destiny*, sailed freely, today's Canal, a UNESCO World Heritage site and popular tourist attraction, remained closed a month past the usual opening date. Boats and barges idled on the Canal's exposed bottom to maintain drinking water levels for the 220,000 inhabitants of surrounding towns.

Mud

boats lounge
in the canal mud

no travel replaces
slow travel

an ocean and a sea
once joined in reverie

no longer meet

My father, Joe Pramik, readying the soil for spring planting in Ohio.

Letter to My Father

France

July 5, 2005

Dear Daddy,

The sunflowers smell like cantaloupes in the rain. Acres—no, miles—of sunflower fields, all saluting east, line both banks of the Canal du Midi, the waterway built four centuries ago to connect the Atlantic Ocean and the Mediterranean Sea. They remind me of your full summer garden with its border of these sentinel plants. Here I am in France and you, at 88, are recovering in Ohio from three recent bouts of pneumonia, a collapsed lung, and the confusion that illness sometimes brings.

In so many ways, though, you are with me on this journey. Walking along the canal this morning, a deluge quickened my strides. At a run, the sunflowers on my right blended with the rain to fill the air with the essence of melon. The musky atmosphere also reminded me of how you courted the cantaloupes in your garden in May. You would gently lift their delicate tendrils from under the thicker vines, rearranging them for growth, and ordered your five children not to traverse the melon section of the quarter-acre plot.

We usually obeyed this command because in late July you would call us into the kitchen to share in an especially exquisite melon. You waited until it had fallen from the vine of its own accord. As if in a religious procession, you carried it to the kitchen counter. Next, you sacrificed it with your sharpest knife, filling the air with a sweetness not often found in today's market fruits. You scooped the abundant wet seeds from the center, sliced thin slivers, and placed one each into our tiny, upturned hands. The deep orange-pink of the flesh delighted your five small congregants. As in a ritual benediction, we would silently eat the melon to the rind. You would then collect the seeds from this one melon and dry and store them along with the memory and hope for more of the sweetest next year.

You would have meandered through the Saint-Albans Sunday Market all morning, past the vendors with your arms folded, head slightly cocked, judging each grower by the fruits of their labors. Sunday in Toulouse, with its bright clear sunlight and crystal crisp air, found us, however, bareheaded, marching in disarray to the weekly farmers' market. We walked through the streets along the canal to Saint-Albans' church with its beige towers and fortress-like straight walls. Encircling this imposing structure was stall after stall brimming with local fruits and vegetables. The aubergines had a high-gloss sheen that reflected each other as the middle-aged gentleman piled them gently in a high pyramid. We wandered through each row as it braided itself around the edge of the old church. Long loaves of freshly baked bread lined the tables on our right while flower stalls punctuated our left. We admired the small fragrant strawberries in their wood-slat baskets.

Our mission was to gather vegetables for our week on the canal aboard the *Royal Destiny*, the cruiser rented for our writers' journey down the waterway. We bought a head of cauliflower as wide as a dinner plate and long, pungent white-tipped radishes. Heads of lettuce and cantaloupes seemed to climb into our sacks. We stopped at the dried herb and spice stand just to enjoy the earthy fragrance of anise and other weedy-looking bouquets. I bought a straw hat that would come into service later on the canal. But we had to return to the boat after an hour to meet our cast-off schedule.

The Canal du Midi is about as wide as Wheeling Creek in some places as our creek winds through the valleys of Jug Run and Slag Hill and Blaine toward the Ohio River. It winds past more poetic places like Mont-giscard, Laval, Écluse d'Encassan, Laurens, and Écluse de la Domergue on its path to the Mediterranean Sea. Wheeling Creek has its peculiar orange and gray-brown murkiness depending on the seasonal runoff, but the Canal keeps its solid green color throughout the year.

As we motored quietly along after cast-off, I wondered what we would have done had our Ohio creek been blocked up with locks—single, double, or even six at a time. So far south of the Erie Canal, with its own lock system, we missed the rhythm of the waterway. Landlocked in Ohio, we had little chance to develop boating skills for navigating the narrow streams as they do in France. Lock keepers live year-round in assigned cottages to maintain the locks and allow boats passage. Several of the lock keepers cultivate flowering gardens, some with exotic and some with native plantings. Each lock had its own personality, it seemed.

Our first evening found us moored at Écluse Montgiscard. *Écluse* is the French word for "*lock.*" As the boat rocked so gently that I soon did not even notice the motion, I sat on the deck and watched the swallows glide and swoop overhead. With their distinctive, black-tipped tails held proudly aloft, the white birds dove toward the yellow-green canal waters, sliced the surface, then soared into the pink-tinged evening sky. They carried on an energetic banter among each other—a screaming, "peep-peep-peep" that seemed to say, "ready or not, here I come with reckless abandon, ha ha." Over and over and over again, it was a nonstop ballet for over an hour. This contrasted mightily with the behavior of us humans on the boat who sat with our notebooks and pens, thinking about writing. Not a peep. We were motionless while the swallows performed a continuing aerial dance. Their enthusiasm moved me to want to join them as they so enjoyed their glides and pirouettes.

Glancing toward the destination of their dives, I saw a different kind of dance. Stick-thin, almost imperceptible water striders zigzagged over the hazy green canal surface. They seemed to be holding a convention on this section of the canal. Dressed in their yellow-backed bodies with black lines and legs, I observed some astride each other in homage to their short summer lifespan. They continued their mating ritual and hoped the swallows would miss them on the next dive.

The vegetation in France, where I know you never visited, is very similar to that of Ohio, with the plane trees, locusts, maples, and oaks. I pressed a representative leaf of each in my notebook, which brought back memories of elementary school when I would walk through the woods behind our home to collect samples to label. The plane trees are anything but plain. They bow toward each other from the complementary shore to form a leafy archway under which we pass. Their roots stand exposed at the waterline, resembling the talons of birds holding their prey. I saw several families of ducks hiding this year's new hatchlings under rooty grids of the plane trees.

The locust trees responded to touch just as those trees did outside Grandma's summer kitchen. An almost imperceptible pressure as my finger neared the oval leaves would raise the alarm along the thin branch. The leaves would recoil in mad succession, alerting the adjacent foliage as if my finger were tinged with poison.

However, nowhere have I seen fields of cultivated sunflowers other than in Southern France. There was an aura of sheer joy in the miles and miles of ten- and twelve-foot-high bobbing flowers. You would plant at most two rows of these starchy-stemmed plants at the bottom end of your garden. But the French seem to thrive on their yellow-brown blossoms. You could almost hear the flowers laugh from the fields as we motored past.

The French cook much like your Polish family did. The food here is just what you would order since you were the meat-and-potatoes member of the family. However, you and I share a love of seafood, and I so wished you could have shared the seafood *grillé* with its scallops, fish, and shrimp in a butter sauce with Parmesan that I ordered last night at dinner. You would have polished the baking dish with the walnut artisan bread that brought back the texture and aroma of Grandma's—your mother's—Sunday rolls. This loaf tasted like each ingredient was lovingly selected and added one at a time and kneaded into the dough with determination yet grace. You would have cracked those walnuts. Your mother would have just said, in her native Polish, of course, walnuts we need. And you would have run off to the fruit cellar burrowed into the hill behind your house and pulled out the sack of walnuts you had collected the previous August. Expert at whatever you do, you would have filled the Mason quart jar full of nuts in less than a quarter-hour, returning to the lower kitchen with your contribution to the bread.

At the town of Montesquieu-Lauragais, above Écluse Negre where we moored our boat, the *Royal Destiny*, I was stopped by two gardens after our mile climb up a country road. These two rectangular plots felt so much like home in the evening, so like your meditative space where we would watch you out of the corners of our eyes, as you hoed rhythmically in the darkening summer sky. We ate at a restaurant called The Old Oven. After dinner, the rain poured down, and the kind cook and owner drove us on two trips back to the boat.

I just want you to know that, though I am far away, you are with me. I think about the someday of your death constantly, and Mommy's, and about how I will feel when I become an orphan in this world. The Canal du Midi, *une vie aparte*, seems to stop time, however. To be here in the now and live each day is what you with your quiet ways seemed to teach us all the while as we focused on growing up and moving on. At first, we were all busy with school, then finding a place to be on this earth, and then raising our families in other places. I somehow believed you would always be there, each spring and summer, tending your garden, raising the tomatoes for Mommy's special spaghetti sauce. Strong and alert, you would wait for me to return home to ask you how best to plant the bell peppers and how close to space the corn plants, and how best to live this life through. Now that I have a moment, I find that you no longer have the energy for your first garden. Brother Joe planted five tomato plants, and a friend brought over three bell pepper starters to keep the land alive. Now, much of your time you spend in quiet dreaming between the life before and the hereafter. When I return from this trip, I will come and sit by you and listen to your dreaming. And then, I will walk out into the summer heat and water the garden.

Love,
Mary Jean

FACT: In 2023, France is experiencing severe drought conditions as is much of central Europe and Italy. Repetitive droughts wreak havoc on water levels in lakes and rivers. Southern France cultivates the vibrant fruits and vegetables—apples, tomatoes, strawberries, hazelnuts, plums, and walnuts—we see in European markets.

Reflection

an empty ribbon
  rivers
    then lakes

neighbors no longer
  share berries

desiccated
  fields

Cavorting with a colony of gentoo penguins in Antarctica expanded my love of traveling, even if the odor was overwhelming!

Pilgrimage to the Ice Continent

Antarctica

*If one is standing still and bareheaded and exhales
a deep breath, one can actually hear one's breath
freezing a moment or two after it has left the mouth.
What one hears I do not precisely know... The sound
itself is not easy to describe; it is rather like that
produced by the movement of sand on a beach when
a wave washes up.*

—Captain Robert F. Scott,
Voyage of the Discovery (1901-1904)

Blinding glare. I felt my pupils shrink to pinpoints. Jagged breath clawed its way down my throat and lungs as minute ice crystals ripped the pink tissue. Blue iridescent surfaces and dazzling white glaciers surrounded me, seeming to embed themselves in my chest. The air temperature was a balmy 32 degrees Fahrenheit.

Stunned, thrilled, and in acute pain, my breath caved inward. I nearly fell forward down a glacial slide.

I felt an instant full-body brain freeze. In a mental fog that often accompanies a pounding illness, I suffered immediate joy and an *oh-shit* nanosecond puncture of my conscious mind.

I stood, a tiny person, a pinpoint in a vermillion parka, scaling the forty-five degree slope of a glacier—my initiation to Antarctica.

I'd begun a quest to this mass of ice and rock as my first solo pilgrimage. Antarctica defined "getting away from it all." A white continent with few human inhabitants and many exotic creatures—the albatross, the penguin, the blue whale. After the recent collapse of my twenty-five year marriage and the launch of three fledgling solo adults, I set out to explore the world. I watched my 91-year-old father sink into old age; I knew I had to jump aboard my new life and cast off. Now or never.

Guilt dragged my spirit over the coals of irresponsibility. I was leaving my father in the hands of four younger siblings though I bore the responsibility as the eldest, the matriarch of our small clan from rural Ohio. On the flight toward the South Pole, I worried my father would die while I tramped over the Antarctic ice. "Enjoying myself" floated through my mind.

I'd watched my father smile at the activities of the birds around the backyard birdfeeder. The fowl antics explained the entire world to him, he told me. Juncos, wrens, tits, cardinals, and Baltimore orioles jostled for space on the eighteen-inch-long feeder. Small birds nudged feathered creatures twice their size off the wooden perches. Woodpeckers sounded in the trees farther back across the fence. My father could watch the backyard goings-on, the flits over the porch railings for hours it seemed. He came from a simple, straightforward world dictated by a Farmers' Almanac philosophy of life: dig the soil at first thaw, plant potatoes in March, followed by tomatoes, then lettuce, beets, peppers. Harvest and can the vegetables in June, July, August. Field lies fallow in September with a few straggler tomatoes and pumpkins populating the garden in October. Allow some to rot as fertilizer for the coming spring. Spread winter straw. Repeat in January.

I left him gazing out the dining room window at the snow-covered ground in February. Smiling at his avian menagerie and winter quiet.

"I'll bring back bird stories for you, Dad," I said.

"Good, good. Tell me how they behave down there—if they're any different than here," he said.

His short-term dementia faded in and out. He could describe vivid events about his eight-year-old self but not recall what he'd had for breakfast. On one level, I felt that he knew I'd embarked on my own quest, much later in life than his plunging into the Pacific War zone in his late twenties. I felt a quiet blessing from him; he didn't have to state it outright.

I landed in Buenos Aires, Argentina, and then connected to the nearly three-hour flight to Ushuaia, the frontier town where I would rendezvous with my Quark Expeditions ship, Ocean Nova, to Antarctica. From the Ushuaia lodge, I checked in with a brother by email. Dad still sat, and sometimes stood, by the window enjoying his bird world at home. I'd be without communications with Ohio for forty-eight hours or more as the eighty-passenger Ocean Nova plunged into the tumultuous Drake Passage.

During the two-day crossing, I contracted bronchitis and an energy-draining viral infection. Nearly every passenger developed a hacking cough, with the majority experiencing some degree of seasickness as well. I was spared the latter condition. The ship's physician kindly gave me his last half-bottle of Robitussin.

Two days after anchoring on the Antarctic Peninsula, a skittering ride in a Zodiac skiff deposited me onto a glassy blue glacier. The Ocean Nova anchored on the horizon. I'd ventured so far from eastern Ohio. Despite my high temperature, racking cough, and searing lungs, nothing could stop me from scaling the mountain of ice before me.

Step. Pole. Step. Pole. Step. Pole. Each frigid inhalation sliced deeper into my lungs. I could hear the lining of my bronchi scream. Plodding in my boots, rooted in the ice, was the only way forward. My ID tag fell onto the snow. I retrieved it. With each lurch ahead, I inched further from the heartbreak of home, closing in on my newfound self as an "explorer." I had no option but to climb to the top ledge as instructed by the landing leader. The Zodiac crew coughed and sniffled nearby. Acutely responsible for each of their charges, these wildly fantasizing adventurers hailed from all over the globe: United States, China, Japan.

When I revisit the photographs from that ascent, I'm always shocked that I am beaming, actually grinning, every step of the way. When under acute duress, members of the kingdom Animalia often respond with extremely odd actions. Like my father returning to the coal mine in January to support his family. Displacement behavior, animal scientists call it. I knew I would stand in this place only once in my lifetime. I wasn't about to let a case of bronchial pneumonia and viral infection stop my exploration, dammit.

Fever boiled inside my body. I removed the bulky parka. I was sweating—wet sweat. A brisk wind shrieked through the silence as I reached the top of the ridge overlooking the bay. The glacier walls towered majestically over the cerulean water and chunks of floating ice.

Just then, the glacier calved. What ecstasy! Before me, huge masses of ice, each the size of a house, a ship, a cathedral, a skyscraper, and all combined heaved and crashed into the sea. Witnessing, through tears, this natural marvel of a glacier giving birth elevated me out of my body. My shipmates cheered! I teetered above the ledge, my breath stilled.

The next days, filled with disembarkations to several gentoo and Adélie penguin colonies, conjured stories I would soon tell my father. The Ocean Nova troop visited these rookeries late in the hatching season. Odor, or "stench" as some of my shipmates labeled the smells, clawed at the air, entering our nostrils and clothing, clinging there for weeks afterward. The smells rivaled cattle and hog slaughter yards throughout the Midwest.

Our guides instructed us to stay five feet away from the nesting creatures, which proved virtually impossible because penguin chicks harbor no fear of humans. Young fledglings waddled up and surrounded me if I stood still for a photo. The screech and roar of the colony imprinted itself in my memory, echoing upon our return to the ship.

During one such stop, one gentoo youngster seemed acutely distraught, running to and fro, shrieking about something terrible. I went into parent mode. I felt called to intervene. *There, there, little guy. What's the matter? Mom or Dad will return soon.* I so wanted to hug the little creature to comfort him or her.

Later, conversing with one of the American field biologists who actually camp out several days within the colony, she said she and her two colleagues attempted to count the penguins in each colony. She estimated about six hundred fledglings (not including the two parents of each who were out fishing to feed their offspring). Actual counting proved difficult, the biologist noted. Her team would notch the numbers to about three hundred, then "all hell" would rip through the colony as a predatory skua would attack a chick or dive at a nest. The next moment, all the penguins would scurry around frantically with parents attempting to protect their fledgling or their egg. Family life at these penguin stops seemed much like my upbringing in Ohio. Anything could upset the calm of our household. My aged father would love this story and the hundreds of photos of the penguin chicks covered in blood and guano.

In sharp contrast to the hysteria of the penguin colony, one day I found myself listening to ice crackling in a lagoon off the western side of the Antarctic Peninsula. This brash ice sang a joyful noise in the sunlit air. I sat in the Zodiac, that black tuberous flotation device, with seven other puffy-clad humans. We were warm and comfortable. No one spoke. Cold whispered against chapped cheeks, our eyes rested behind dark glasses, the constant rhythmic crackling sounds rocked us like a lullaby. Brash ice also sounds like glass shattering, with the volume turned up high. A seal floating on a slab of ice nearby moaned a greeting. Mid-lagoon, no scent arose from the cold. The crackling ice was all-encompassing, surround sound over which I had no control. This precious din would continue forever, weather permitting. Brash ice compares to Rice Krispies popping in a darker key or a dissonant marimba needing tuning. It's actually the sound of ancient ice melting, glacial air bubbles escaping their centuries-old prison. Under a cloudless sky, the water reflected a deep shade of black-lavender, floating between gigantic cliffs of white and gray so bright and luminescent that my eyes hurt. Frigid breaths, inhaled deep, deep into my lungs. The cold hurts, hurts, I thought. A gentoo penguin chorus riffed on a distant ice floe. On an existential level, we lost our relationship with deep time as the ice melted. Sitting amid the brash ice, I heard the symphony of ancient air sacs enlivening the universe.

On the final stop before reentering the Drake Passage to return to Ushuaia and the voyage home, we disembarked at Whalers Bay on aptly named Deception Island. It testified to the intensity of the international whaling industry from a bygone era. Whaling factory ships were prominent in the early 1900s and played a large role in killing off more than fifty thousand whales in the late 1930s. I was heartbroken to hear this. The sadness of such a massive kill was still palpable at the site. In 1986, the International Whaling Commission banned commercial whaling to replenish the world's whale populations. But Whalers Bay, with its abandoned dilapidated buildings, whale carcasses, and wrecks of boats and ships, projected an eerie atmosphere. The loneliness of the abandoned souls still wrestling among the rocks and empty structures hung over the site. They spoke a silent lament to the killing of these majestic creatures.

From the warm waters of Whalers Bay, we hiked up the dormant volcano to Neptune's Window, the lookout over the Bellinghausen Sea. Black lava nuggets were interspersed upward on the solid rock. By this time, my strength had returned, and the raving lung infection quieted. It was as if the sights and sounds of ice and snow cast healing energy on us all. I no longer needed the heavy down parka.

At the top of the ridge, I probed the translucent wall forming the cliffs of Deception Island. White ice lunged out of dark waters into the turquoise blue sky. Then I sighted her. A lone Adélie penguin stood on a small ledge hundreds of feet about the water. How did she alight there on that ice shelf? Penguins don't fly, though they can propel themselves through the air when menaced by a predator in the water. She had no way down to the water or up to the safety of the ridge.

At this moment, I felt the singularity of my life. Much like this solitary Adélie. This image has remained with me over the many years since my pilgrimage to the ice continent. It connected with the email received on my return to Ushuaia. My father was in hospice, fading fast. A mere two weeks from the start of my journey. I made haste to return to Ohio.

One week after leaving Antarctica, I held my father's hand for the last five days of his life. In his final breath, his hand still warm in mine, a blinding flash of iridescent blue light, like the Antarctic glaciers I'd spent weeks with, flew off to my right. Nanosecond-quick, did I really see what I thought I saw? There's no instant replay in life. Time does not march on; it fleets, it zaps, it exhales...it's gone.

I didn't tell him about my explorer's journey, didn't tell him of the glorious creatures I'd met, didn't tell him about their cavorting joy, and didn't paint for him the picture of life on ice. In my mind's eye, I see myself at times as the solo Adélie penguin on that ledge on Deception Island. I hold onto that image. The strength gained by experiencing and enduring the tribulations of the pilgrimage to Antarctica gave me the strength to bid my father farewell.

FACT: Antarctic ice mass has diminished by 149 billion metric tons of ice per year over the past two decades, contributing to the rise in the world's sea level. Recent modeling studies predict a "rapid and unstoppable" sea level increase by 2050 that will continue for hundreds of years into the future—even if kept at the target increase of two degrees Celsius.

Melting

Brash ice
  singing
after
birth of
calved ice

shelf
  melting
  into the sea
   its final weather
   we

The ill-tempered melteme, the extreme wind from the
Aegean north, gathers force at night.

The Winds of Mesochori

Greece

The knock at the weathered door startled the breakfast circle. It was Yiannis, Virginia's neighbor.

"Is Mary Jean here?" asked the quiet-spoken Greek gentleman. "I have found her passport blowing and tumbling in the wind." Yianis' extended hand gently presented the thin blue book.

The gusty *melteme*, an unusual wind for the Peloponnesus summer, had played with my paper identity along the dusty red-clay road near the arched entry to Virginia's retreat. I had not yet missed this essential document, having just arrived the day before at a writer's workshop on the southern tip of Greece.

We had settled at the Vatika village in Mesochori on a hot humid Monday afternoon. Traveling for five hours by freeway from Athens, then country roads to reach Neapolis, the van had crawled past the gray aging ruins of the Ottoman (or Venetian) fort. I realized why my travel research had not found any mention of this mountainside hamlet. Mesochori, once an important contributor to Vatika's district government, now hangs on the edge of a carved, virtually vertical hill. Vatika's "balcony" watches over the growing town of Neapolis, centered on concave Vatika Bay.

I had come to Greece searching for a respite to mend my tired spirit. My mother had died several months earlier, and I needed some peace and solace from my grinding American life to continue the grieving process. I needed the space to decide which memories to keep, which to discard. Friends offered comfort of sorts; they advised that each person must complete the first difficult, yet vital, year of mourning the loss of a parent to move on to the next stage of living.

My work responsibilities had granted me a few weeks off to set family needs in order, but I turned to my daily frenzied work schedule, sidestepping the void of holidays, my mother's first missed birthday, the reflex of phoning every Saturday morning with the week's summary of news. My youngest child's college applications, auditions, and teenage rebellion had packed the year with further chaotic activity so that I could legitimately ignore any residual sadness. My aching muscles and listless spirit petitioned for time alone near the seaside for cleansing and rest. An effusive Greek-American friend residing in Athens dangled a compelling offer of a writers' workshop near the southern seaside town of Neapolis.

Thus, I stand in the here and now of Mesochori with a kind stranger.

"*Efcharisto poli kala*," was my grateful reply in

limping Greek for the prevented days at the U.S. Embassy.

Yiannis—John in his adopted city of Vancouver, British Columbia—embraced my hand. He recalled for us how he had not returned to his birth village of Mesochori for sixty years. However, when the sinking global economy reached his Canadian engineering firm and forced his retirement, he and his wife decided to revisit these sunlit mountains.

"I felt at home. I had grown up in Mesochori and attended high school in Neapolis. I felt I belonged." Yiannis looked down at his weathered hands as he joined the group for coffee. He recounted his days as an engineer in the far western province of Canada, where his company signed on to the global quest for profits, bought and sold so many times that he "retired" earlier than he had expected. His engineering and architectural skills facilitated his building an exquisite, white-walled three-story home at the outer edge of Mesochori, where he lived with Mary, his wife, for six months each year.

As we continued in quiet conversation, Yiannis told of his memory loss, a topic always on his mind, it seemed. It was as if he keeps it at the front and center of his cerebral cortex lest he forget himself.

"I remember the important things," he said almost in reverie. He remembered his love for his wife, his native land, his daughter, and two dear grandsons, the thought of the latter bringing a broad smile to his eyes. He remembered how to set tomatoes and zucchini in the red-clay garden on the hillside in Mesochori each spring.

As he spoke, I began to remember too. I experienced memory loss as well, from a traumatic divorce at a time of my own aging, becoming a single parent unintentionally and an orphan unexpectedly. At times, I searched through the set synaptic pathways that had once been so keen and thorough. I often did not find what I was looking for immediately. Then, days later, the face, the name, the flower, the poem surfaced as if to surprise me with the joy of knowing that this essence of a day from my life remained as though hidden in a cave.

"I think my memory loss is from the world moving too fast, from the computers making things so jumbled at times." Yiannis' gaze connected with mine. I sat upright. That sentiment had often crossed the diasporic web that had become my mind.

Yiannis moved on to another connection.

"These winds are very unusual. They are more than the *melteme*." He reckoned that climate change had created havoc with weather everywhere, even here in the sacred precinct of southern Greece. He related his experience of the "disaster winds" that sped down from the northern country at one hundred miles per hour a few years before, a wind that overturned boats in Vatika Bay.

"I watched as it blew off the side of my garage here. It just sheared the wall," he recounted.

I returned to the night of our arrival: temperatures well over 95 degrees Fahrenheit and a ferocious swirling rain pounding the red-tiled roof of our retreat. The ill-tempered *melteme* rattled the worn unpolished shutters at their iron latches. Huddled inside the white walls, I felt each gust lunge up the precipitous hillside as if an angry god determined to slay trees, olive and fig, and the chaparral not rooted deeply in the earth. Bending tightly, I held my knees close to form a ball. I imagined the trees trying to protect their fruits from this thieving wind. Where did the ubiquitous cicadas and grasshoppers seek shelter on such a night?

Leaves burst under the door, resembling multi-colored scorpions. Centipede-like creatures appeared on the hanging towels. Sparrows sang and cicadas rasped in rhythm despite the colossal drafts that blasted up the mountain from the waters below. Lying in the dense darkness, I waited for the squall to pass. For three days and nights, I waited along with the tankers and boats anchored in Vatika Bay, too timid to challenge Poseidon's lashes. It was as if this *melteme* wanted all to know who controlled our travels. Not the Greek deity Hermes, who would have hovered over us several thousand years ago, nor the saints or our schedules.

The next day, a lull allowed a meditative amble around the mountainside villages of Mesochori, Faraklo, and Lachi. The gentle, lightened pace of Greek time created a cavernous echo of thought. I imagined hearing voices from the hermits, the shepherds, and the sailors and their widows on the shore who had wandered this land eons ago. Abandoned brown-gray stone corpses of ancient buildings leaned comfortably against the whitewashed new limestone and marble structures that speckled the cliffside villages. Hiking through Mesochori and onward to the next town of Faraklo, I wondered what histories and myths lay buried in these empty structures with no roofs and windowpanes with no glass. These hollowed-out buildings raised the thought of my mother's emptied bureau and my father's request to leave the clothes inside "because somebody may need them someday." Ageless voices seem to whisper, "How do we live through time?" This land of Vatika, with its vast army of buried memories of so many wars, massacres, and crusades, was a legend of an underwater city that anchored the bay.

Angled some five hundred feet above the sea-level town of Neapolis, Mesochori connects to civilization via a dirt road with alternating sections of challenging blacktop switchbacks not for the faint of heart. Wild cicadas screamed during the sunlight hours, and a lonely rooster punctuated any random moment of the day. The white Church of Christ's Transfiguration stood closed, damaged by an earthquake years ago. The nearby graveyard hosted twenty-seven above-ground graves in the Greek Orthodox tradition. Several graves housed husbands and wives who lived together for more than half a century and now remained so in eternity.

Resting on the stairs behind the church, I begin to understand why a sojourn in Greece was so necessary at this time in my life. An accepting country with wide-open-armed people provided fertile ground for the metamorphosis whose time had come. I discover a cicada exoskeleton littering the ground. If it were only so easy for us larger multi-celled creatures to shed a tiresome persona or a no-longer-useful survival pattern! Caught up in a midlife of tumultuous change, lost husbands, broken promises, departing parents, and escaping children who were off to new galaxies that a parent would never see, the moment of transformation beckoned. I seemed to be in the process of reinventing myself in every moment, at times with nanometer transmutations, at other moments through battering by a wild wind like the *melteme*.

I carefully stored my passport. I continued to consider how I could remember more of who I really am. Perhaps the adventurous five-year-old who challenged her small-town existence when the world seemed ever so big and exciting remained somewhere at my center. But the fresh college graduate who hitch-hiked across the country to California at 22 because that place defined the edge of the world lay dormant like a protected spore.

In looking for myself, it was indeed fitting that I lost my passport. Yet it was returned to me by a gentle man who at another point on this planet had experienced thoughts synchronous with mine. These days had allowed me the time to consider who I am in the present moment. Would I return a changed woman? Would I better process the loss of a mother I could not please and change how I expressed my love for my children? They asked for unconditional love, the *agape* of acceptance of their humanity and their missteps. My current life required that I listen to a son's rap music, four-letter words and all, hearing these songs that paralleled the music of the Sixties. It demanded valuing the middle child's painful mistakes, allowing them to take on a new luster like that of her all-encompassing smile. It meant appreciating the oldest child's tenacity and elegance as it shined on her deep grace and creative power at her own pace. Shedding a brittle outer core would require creating the time to feel the Greek *parea* of being in community, a time for friends.

Perhaps Yiannis was correct that the speed and frenetic nature of our Western existence prevent us from remembering the habits of kindness and love that spring spontaneously from the fully present Greek. Like Yiannis, I felt more at home here than in the United States. As I walked the road to Mesochori and sat and shared ouzo or tea with friends, I felt more alive. I no longer held my breath awaiting the next moment.

Finding the time to change can be daunting at best. But sometimes life forces the issue as it has over my past few years. Here I watched several Greek women who daily manifested the courage to be themselves. From moment to moment, I still felt like a leaf running on the wind, tossed about in inelegant disarray. On some days, I felt like the wind itself. A solid passport contained only a piece of one's identity. It wasn't who I am. From my study of science, I knew that no facts remain static for long. New experiences, new experiments will liquefy any dogma. Unceasing wisdom grows on this earth.

Metamorphosis continues. Unrelenting. Movement is constant. Greece was the appropriate place for me at that moment. I could feel the spiritual carapace cracking down my back. The time approached to step out of the door and room that confined me. A time to rejoin the winds.

FACT: Devastating wildfires burned hundreds of thousands of forest acres in recent years. Greece, known for its antiquities, plans to cut dependence on fossil fuels and wean itself off indigenous lignite for electricity. To reduce climate change challenges, it established the Ministry for the Climate Crisis and Civil Protection in 2021 in acceptance that "the climate crisis is already here. It's real." Indeed.

Cassandra

Ionian sirens swirl and
gift the Corinthian
                    blue sea

        roiling waters
            flood ancient ruins

    pearling
            a newborn
        catastrophe

Played here with a bone-like stick, the single-frame bodhran drum is a favorite of small groups playing in Dublin pubs.

The Drummer's Heart

Ireland

As the Irish are wont to say, the musicians smoked a jig our first night at O'Donoghue's Pub, the epicenter of Irish music, on Dublin's Merrion Row. Cloistered in the front corner of the wood-paneled watering hole in the middle of the city, John Walsh organized his song list in his head. Against the dusky wall in the center of the musical ring sat Jose with a bodhran (bow-rahn), the Irish open drum. Right, Jose is not a very Irish name. Hailing from Spain, he said he just liked the sound of the instrument and had practiced enough to join in.

"Waltons' factory, here in Dublin, you can find a good bodhran for three hundred euros," Jose whispered to me as he passed by.

I'm sensitive to drums. Often the windows on my San Francisco home bulge and shake. Not from earthquakes but from reverberations walloped out by my son Josef's practice on his full drum kit and assorted tympani: bass, two toms, snare, and a radiant array of speckled cymbals. He practices on a flat rubber pad to "tighten his chops." Orange Styrofoam earplugs securely in place, he extemporizes for hours with eyes semi-shut. To date, no police car has pulled into the driveway nor has a neighbor disparaged the whole lot of shakin' that does go on.

One of Josef's mystified high school teachers, however, once asked me, "How can you stand his practicing?" She was definitely not a parent. My answer required only a second of reflection.

"But it's music," I said matter-of-factly. And it is.

Josef's drumming has taken on a healing rhythm over the last several years. Mickey Hart, drummer for the Grateful Dead, offered that drumming heals the soul to a packed Grace Cathedral one Sunday in San Francisco. Josef sat in rapt attention in the front pew, inhaling Hart's words.

When I travel, I am always alert to a new drum opportunity for Josef. On Jose's Dublin tip, I began to search for the perfect bodhran. Not the tourist contraption with a stenciled Irish scene on the head, serving up dissolute sound. I had come to Ireland on a quest for the modern Irish soul. If I had not yet located that spiritual center, I had surely tripped onto the country's musical heart. In the fuchsia-laden innocence that is rural Ireland—County Cork—I began my search for the special bodhran, a birthday gift for Josef.

The open frame bodhran sets the heartbeat of Irish music. A large circle of wood, capped at one end by a smooth sheath of sheepskin, the drummer cradles the bodhran under his or her arm and hugs it tight against the body while sensually massaging the taught skin from the inside. With the other hand, the musician twiddles the double-headed beater or tipper against the outside surface.

A skilled bodhran player is a prized find for traditional Irish music groups. This frame drum is an exciting instrument in the right hands, layering a subtle sound to Irish folk music. To the untrained ear, the bodhran appears to be an easy path into a band and free pub ale. Not so, however, because the bodhran player must work to match the tune and the melody.

As one of Josef's music teachers explained it, "The drummer does not keep the rhythm. The drummer paints; he fills in the spaces of absence."

I had always thought otherwise: Drummer equals beat.

"Not so, Mom," said Josef. "The bassist keeps the beat."

"Oh." Learn something new every day.

Church bells pealed eventide as we entered the Armada Pub in Kinsale, County Cork. The chatter of the skittle evoked the serenity of the crowd at the Armada Pub. With that heavenly accent Irish barmaids have patented, the waitress with emerald eyes asked, "What can I get ya?" The fetid scent of the room smelled of many a spilled whisky.

As we settled into the bitterness of the night's first

sip of stout, the musicians sitting at the round table in the center of the room stoked their instruments. Balding and wiry, plumber Fenton Healy orgasmically twisted his body, caressing the bodhran while beating out the tune with either his hand or his baby-rattle-shaped tipper. Busker Ian MacLean, dreadlocks pulled back in a ponytail, plunked the banjo, and biotech engineer Sean Pol O Cathain raked widespread fingers over his American-made John Allen accordion. Led by Diarmyid Grod, a professional guitarist, they barreled through reels, jigs, waltzes, and all music Irish through-out the evening. But of course, my eyes keyed in on Fenton who, sporting a pale mustache, cocked his head to and fro much like a rooster in the farmyard as he smacked the beat on his bodhran.

This starry night celebrated the first time they were all playing together, said accordionist Sean Pol. What good fortune for us pub patrons as the four young fellows spoke to our spirit. So inspired, I continued my search for that bodhran in earnest. After all, Josef was one-quarter Irish by birth. A bodhran he should play.

Back at the Bellevue B&B in Myrtleville, I turned to the internet. Why not find the bodhran online so I would not have to haul a suspect round shape through the nightmare security at Heathrow on my return?

I could easily pick up a bodhran at the Waltons Musical Instrument Galleries on Frederick Street in Dublin and ship it to San Francisco to arrive in time for Josef's birthday. Brilliant. I fired off an email. Pascal

Sallou of the Waltons Music marketing team zipped a reply after his return from a long weekend:

"We don't really ship items to the U.S. as we have a distributor down there. I'd suggest that you contact them; they'll help you."

I fired back: "I am a romantic. Buying the bodhran for my son's nineteenth birthday on the fifth of July in Dublin, Ireland, would be lovelier than a U.S. distributor. Thank you. Please: Do you have a sixteen-inch tunable maple bodhran?" Pascal must have considered my frenzied request just another one of those crazy American queries. He did not reply to that last missive.

Several hamlets and taverns later, I happened upon a magic circle of musicians at Buckleys pub in Crosshaven, Cork. The warm community oozed through the tight quarters. Buckleys' smiling owner, Nina Casey, with her bob of short gray hair and crisp black-and-white-striped shirt, served as high priestess, deftly delivering drinks to one and all.

The musicians that night at Buckleys underlined for me how my son could feel a well-loved part of a family when playing in such company. Several years after the breakup of our family, Josef explained how he made it through the ensuing years in his college essays. He went for "truth" rather than "essays for the Ivy League."

"School became harder, family activities became scarce, and my life sometimes felt like everything was crashing down. This is when I turned to music to help me through this time. Jazz became my new dinner table as Art Blakey, Jackie McClean, and Josef Zawinul filled the plates, utensils, pots, and pans... All I want to do now is play music because it is what makes me happy. Writing music, playing music, even practicing, is something I want to do. Once my parents separated, they each became busier, and I had to find new ways to entertain myself, which music did so effortlessly and completely. Finding something I was passionate about taught me how to dig deeper in all of my studies." Josef had written from his heart.

I focused my listening at Buckleys. Jimmy, the bodhran player, also clacked two slender, curved deer bones resembling spoons. Rhythmically twirling them like miniature batons with staccato wrist movements in midair, he created a spectacular percussive clucking sound.

"The bones are from his first wife," quipped a male patron with a wink at the next table. Ah, the proverbial Irish humor was in high cheer this night.

Jimmy's fellow musicians rounded out the evening with two gentlemen on shimmery guitars. Lucy (her dear parents beaming across the table from me) peppered a lively violin, a substantial young man jammed properly on a box accordion, and another fellow squeezed the uilleann pipes ("uilleann" for elbow) with his arm and elbow to amazing effect. At times, a banjo would appear and join in. Then a random pub patron would burst into song, crooning a heart-rending version of "I have loved you dearly." Mesmerized by the sheer force of the music, I came to understand Josef's reckoning that playing with other musicians indeed creates a family.

During a break in their music-making, Jimmy answered my questions about his bodhran. "Go to Cork and to The Living Tradition music store on MacCurtain Street. It's across the street from Crowley's Music Shop."

The very next day, my last full day in County Cork, I made a beeline for The Living Tradition via an extra taxi ride into the town from Myrtleville.

Locating The Living Tradition proved easy. Selecting the right bodhran did not.

Carl, the youthful shop attendant, began pulling out bodhrans. The shelves hosted at least fifty or a hundred of these wooden circles. Carl, a bodhran player himself, offered me his favorite.

"But this drum that you like has no crosspiece in the back," I objected, new bodhran observer that I was.

"I find the crosspiece limits my motion," said Carl. "I can move my hand all over the skin without it." He began to sound like Josef, who would get this point. He had me when it came to opinions on musical instruments.

While I stewed over the dozen or more bodhrans laid out on the carpeted floor, American-born Brian entered the shop. According to Carl, Brian was a premier bodhran player. Raised in Boston, he now lived in Cork with his mother.

With his silver ear studs and black velvet jacket,

Brian authenticated my choice of bodhran. Both young men took turns playing each drum. Their keen enthusiasm and glee re-created the joy I had seen in Josef's face for any drum. As they shilly-shallied about the quality of each drum played, I heard the deep sensual sound that Josef would find truly soulful. I had found that special bodhran with a unique sound.

"This is the bodhran I would want for myself," said Carl. I believed him. The sound was deep, subtle, resonant.

"Ay, a carnage of bodhrans," laughed Brian, smiling at all the drums randomly populating the shop floor. I offered to help put them away, but the two young gentlemen would hear none of it.

"And which tipper do you want?" asked Carl. "Ya, you must have one of these," he said, answering his own question. "Twenty-two euros! For this exquisite thin stick of richly polished mahogany." He smiled as he lovingly wrapped it tightly in a thin sheet of paper.

Carting the eighteen-inch bodhran home through Heathrow security set my next task. With the aplomb of a spy, I managed to squish my backpack into the bodhran case without ripping the goatskin surface while carrying my laptop under my raincoat. At Heathrow, only *one* carry-on is allowed while the connecting plane permits *two* carry-ons. I accomplished my goal. The Irish faeries were a-smiling.

My flight gently settled toward the gray-green waters of San Francisco Bay, with fog stretched over San Bruno Mountain and the Coast Range framing the western border of the peninsula. I cradled the bodhran in its black padded case. It was my son's nineteenth birthday. Embraces and kisses lured me home from all that was Ireland. His sister and friend had prepared the evening's dinner for my son's starring role, even going so far as to bake and assemble his favorite chocolate-mint-chip ice cream cake.

"A drum, right, Mom? This is getting to be a habit. I can use it with my new compositions. Wait until you hear them." He beamed his usual grin as he zipped open the black bag and soothed the taut surface of the bodhran. He immediately played the bodhran, setting the sound reeling in the room, the same sound I had heard in Cork at The Living Tradition. I then noticed the twists and pulsations of his back muscles, akin to the movements of Fenton Healy in Kinsale and Jimmy at Buckleys in Crosshaven. While I had been busy with life, my son had truly become a drummer, a healer of the sadness that beats in all of us at times.

Later, after ice cream birthday cake and assorted merriment on jet lag, we turned down the lights. Ascending the stairs, I caught sight of the bodhran in my son's bedroom, now a music studio. The bodhran nestled next to his snare, leaning against his Senegalese djembe and the Greek dumbéleki. In the hushed darkness of my return, these inanimate percussion instruments portrayed a family, all different, each with its own sound and joyful to be there, to be present with each other.

FACT: In Ireland, the changing climate has increased the annual surface air temperature since the turn of the nineteenth century. The majority of those living in Ireland also experience increased rainfall, sea-level rise, extreme weather storms, flooding, heat waves, and drought. They won't suffer the 50-degree heat waves or Category 5 hurricanes like other countries, but they may be ill-prepared for economic shocks from climate disasters elsewhere on the planet.

Blind

Dublin busker
sings of a fading
   Hibernian coast

  each rolling tear a
  call to native plants,
    vanished fishing villages

a seaboard devoured
   by the one-eyed Balor
     blinded by
       greed

UNESCO Heritage Site of Puglia with its charming *trulli*
buildings made for a restorative week.

Running in Puglia

Italy

An hour before sunrise on a June morning, Puglia beckoned. As I stepped out into the dark, the blackened narrow meandering streets of Alberobello opened like a labyrinth before my *trullo*. I was determined to maintain my marathon training schedule. Often when traveling, my resolve to keep up my running fast dilutes with the local wines from the previous nights. But not on this trip. Over the years, running for me has become a communication with myself and the earth. Here in Puglia, it became a ritual, like making love to the land at the break of day.

Puglia, the district of southern Italy that fills the rugged heel of the boot-shaped country, stands as the heartland where Mussolini harvested his idea of growing food for the entire country that had become Italy. He intended to create a "breadbasket" for the people. Puglia, an impoverished area far from the fashion centers of northern Italy and five hours away by train from the power seat of Rome, responded. The province now produces tasty durum wheat for semolina, olives and olive oil, vibrant full red wines, and a cornucopia of vegetables and fruits.

Without a map or a GPS device, I turned to follow the road out of Alberobello. Named after two feudal wars, *alberobello* means "tree of war." The town nestles alongside a riverbed on two sloping hills about an hour's drive from the Adriatic port of Bari. The eastern hill houses the modern area of town, while the western hill hosts the *trulli*—thick-walled houses with conical roofs sometimes marked by white-painted zodiac and religious symbols. Clustered in two neighborhoods, Rione Monti and Rione Aia Piccola, both boast national monument status and a UNESCO World Heritage Site designation.

On Alberobello's Via Don Francesco Gigante, I paced past an austere campground. No frills for three euros a night. Scattered hay lay under the automobiles and campers. As I ran up past Via Pasteur in the early morning mist, an elderly man tended geraniums on his balcony, pinching the decaying blossoms, moving slowly from plant to plant.

At the trident crossroads, I turned left on intuition toward the spreading rays cresting on the horizon. I recalled a friend asking on a recent evening, "When will you stop this lifestyle?" He meant the repetitive hours of training required each day to achieve a level of fitness for some unnamed event. I had not thought of it as a lifestyle.

"I don't do lifestyles," I told him. "I try to live a life."

Thrusting again toward the horizon, I recalled the

Academy Award-winning 1981 British film, *Chariots of Fire*. I heard its soaring Vangelis synthesizer score as each foot struck the paved country lane. In the film, the Scottish track phenom Eric Liddell raced over the moors above the sea. In one scene, his sister Jennie worried that her brother's interest in running and training for the 1924 Summer Olympics distracted him from their work as missionaries in China.

Reflecting on his sister's concerns, Liddell commented on his running: "I believe that God made me for a purpose [the mission in China], but He also made me fast, and when I run, I feel His pleasure." Though I am not religious, I understand this sentiment.

Through sports training, I first explored my physical self because my body was my most immediate contact with the earth. I reasoned that my current form is the only body housing my mind and any creative spirit available in this lifetime.

At the end of any race, I experience a curious kick during the last fifty meters. My body grinds into my own personal hyperspeed as I focus on the finish line. There is a joy in this movement I had not previously experienced in my life. My legs turn over faster, I angle toward the finish. No matter how exhausted I felt seconds before, my entire being springs forward and zooms. Zipping over the responsive paved road leading out of Alberobello in the cool morning, I understood how Eric Liddell felt the deity's pleasure in running. Fast I may not be, but the first light cresting over the eastern horizon lifted my feet and worn, tightly fitted running shoes.

In this rock-strewn rough heel of the land that is Puglia, the Italian earth is a deep luscious red, as if it absorbed the blood of ancient Messapians, Greeks, Carthaginians, and Romans. As the light began to open the sky, I avoided a black-spotted, pale-green lizard on the sidewalk. I followed the rising sun past home gardens with tall tomato bushes and zucchini blooming golden yellow, each plot hosting several olive and fig trees. Hummingbirds darted in and out of the blossoms as I passed.

Gliding by the garden center on my left, I inhaled the clay essence of the various-shaped terra cotta pots upended one atop the other, waiting for homes later in the day. Then, I took leave of what resembled a town. Now running at a brisk pace, each step took me farther out into farmlands, past cherry trees pregnant with bright red orbs that perked up like nipples on a breast. Blurring past were the gray stone *trulli* where farmers housed the tools of their trade or stored hay for animals nearby.

The amaranthine earth, redolent with iron and assorted minerals, pulled me toward it with a sensuous primordial beckoning. Chicory caressed the stone fences that lined the road. I could feel the sea in this land residing between the Adriatic and Ionian Seas.

At a "Y" in the road, I first followed the orange arrow identifying *Regione Puglia, Bosco Selva Comunale,* and *Silva Arboris Belli*. With rudimentary Italian and

Latin roots memorized in high school, running during these hours did not require a dictionary. I aimed toward the community forest, the beautiful trees. Pine and a touch of balsa scented the gentle zephyr that meandered through the needles. The morning air cleared my breathing, allowing for a faster pace. Yet another horizontal stone fence bordered the forest of curving trees. Along the roadside, a camper stood in quiet contemplation.

I retraced my course and headed to the right at the "Y" in the direction of the *Az Agricola del Trulli* arrow. More *trulli* hid slightly behind higher flat-stoned fences. In one grove of gray-barked olives, a pyre quietly burned with the smoke snaking along the red soil into the dawn as an unseen Puglian cleared his orchard of debris. A crimson-painted wrought-iron gate stood ajar between stone fences, an open invitation. As the sun rose, the inhabitants began to stir out into their fields, checking tomatoes, onions, artichokes. A lone man in blue pants and a white shirt and cap watered his blooming green peppers, neatly ordered in five long rows. Through the leafy branches of cherry trees that bordered his plot, I watched as he stooped over to tenderly prune each plant, much like my father had done so frequently through his ninety-one years. Watching this farmer flooded me with memories of so many Ohio summer mornings when my father would tend his garden before leaving for work in the coal mines.

The gnarled olive and fig trees extended their branches as I ran toward them, welcoming me. I retraced the roads and crossings back toward Alberobello. Small tractor-like vehicles began to pass slowly. The drivers nodded. Passing a furry-blossomed tree as I neared town, thousands of bees swirled about and dove at the white flowers.

I ran through Piazza Curri past the Basilica de SS Medici down the hill in the new town, past the glorious Cantina restaurant where last night friends and I feasted on succulent *burrata*—ricotta wrapped in fresh mozzarella, a vibrant house wine, and two exquisite desserts, with sugar from the final entry powering my run this morning. Stepping lightly so I would not awaken the inhabitants, I tripped past Piazza Mario Pagano, a former threshing center in the town where farmers brought their harvested wheat and other grains to contribute their local count's required allotment.

For ten mornings during these running meditations, I fell in love with Puglia.

FACT: Fifteen years ago, outdoor temperatures required only a light jacket during morning jogs. The air felt cool and balmy on our cheeks. The average annual temperature in Italy has increased 34 degrees Fahrenheit since the late 1800s. Puglia had prolonged high temperatures during the summer months of 2021, reaching a high of 104 degrees Fahrenheit in some areas. Along with falling productivity, a public health emergency was declared.

Heat

on long runs
    and rambles

fresh air at sunrise
    among the pines

watching the farmer
    hoe his tomatoes, peppers

scented with balsam
    morning memories revive

Barbara, the boxer I met in Costa Rica, just adored everyone.
Until I met Barbara, I had a healthy fear of dogs.

Peaceable Kingdom

Costa Rica

Barbara licked my lower calf. It was love at first sight. Hers.

Costa Ricans love life, family, neighbors, peace, food, and sweets. These themes that permeate this most central of Central American countries blared through the library of travel books mounting on my bedstand, desk, and bookcases. I was enamored of the peace-loving Ticos who disbanded their military in 1948. And they do love their dogs. This fact did not make the travelogue pages. It appeared as a postscript on my Costa Rican host's email.

Don Lenny had offered his small rancho outside of San Jose for a week's writers' workshop in the dry season. His five-page, single-spaced missive about the assorted insects (four thousand species), hideous spiders (tarantulas), and venomous snakes (the elegantly toxic fer-de-lance) did not deter me from prompt enrollment. His description of his pet menagerie did: six dogs— "I'm a cat person," I'd say to anyone offering me their teeth-bared pup to pet—six cats, one fiery-billed aracari (a toucan cousin), eleven parrots, and assorted chickens penned with a barrel-chested white rooster. Lenny casually noted that the canine members attack a new guest with bravado and sport. Not my idea of fun as my left calf still sported the scar from a boxer bite received at age twelve. Did I mention that I'm afraid of dogs? My psyche still feels the stitches. I secretly envied my son's animal-loving DNA and his enthusiastic ability to bathe guide dogs for the blind while I waited in the car for him to finish fluffing up his canine family.

Retrieving me from the Juan Santamaria International Airport at midday, Lenny delivered a greeting that reflected a perfected professor's banter about the land crossed with the full-blown love of an expat. I held on tight as we jerked through San Jose traffic and across Costa Rican country roads. Oh, dear. My journalist's eye spotted dogs on both sides of every road and sidewalk, at least one per meter. Dog density was high, way high. Dogs—medium, small, German shepherds, Dobermans with ears not clipped, yapping Chihuahuas—were everywhere. On the way to Finca Fango de la Suerte, we stopped at the residence of Fleur de Liz, hairdresser to Miss Costa Rica, whose mechanic husband tuned the van we would rent for the week. Did I dare step out of the Kia SUV as three menacing Chihuahuas surrounded us? Chihuahuas aim for the throat, my Hollywood education reminded me. Fleur, dressed in black shorts and a black T-shirt, welcomed us, gushing in Spanish. Via linguistic osmosis and as a guest in her country, I stepped out of the vehicle and prayed. Surprisingly, the dogs charged but stopped six inches away, barking wildly but inserting no teeth into flesh (mine). The teeniest ones sniffed my feet. *Muchas gracias, todos santos.*

When we arrived at Lenny and Joan's rancho, he honked the horn twice, a signal to the occupants. The gate clattered and lurched open. A housekeeper grasped a huge caramel-colored creature. As noted in his email, Lenny's canine tribe came bounding out of nowhere, heaving toward the car. Would the windshield stop them? Another preconception disintegrated: Costa Rica, land of peace. I prayed again.

"Barbara, no! Barbara, no!" barked Lenny in an "I'm bigger than you" tone. "*Gracias, Maria de Jesus,*" he added. "Barbara won't bother you. She just loves people. She's sweet and well behaved. She just loves skin," said Lenny as Barbara explored every inch of my exposed leg with her rough, slimy tongue while the other dogs barked, jumped, and pawed my legs in unison.

Finca Fango de la Suerte served as a haven for rescued pets. American expats Lenny and Joan had earned the reputation of "bring 'em on" where animals were concerned. Some pikers simply followed them home. Others migrated via neighbors, friends, locals, or vets.

The rancho's canine consortium included AKC-registered Barbara, chosen by our hosts because boxers have a reputation for being good with grandchildren—she was sweet-tempered but had an uncontrollable urge to lick skin. "Especially the skin of people she's never met before," Lenny explained as I stood still, enduring the slurps.

Sasha, a British ridgeback—a standard breed in the Central Valley—joined the compound as a puppy as well. Joan and Lenny had stopped at a festival for children. At the adopt-a-pet booth at day's end, Sasha was a leftover. Of course, they had to take her home. "She's passive and sweet, but will not play with the cats. Her pals are Barbara and Tutu." Lenny scratched behind Sasha's left ear. "A German shepherd attacked Sasha one day, pulling her out from under a neighbor's bed. She had eighty stitches on her left ear and the side of her face." Sasha sat and cast her Mona Lisa smile up at me. My fears begin to melt.

Next to arrive was Chiquita, a short-haired fox terrier. Most representatives of this breed that I have known could be classified as "yappers." Not Chiquita; she knew better. She had lived on a palatial Costa Rican estate that housed a zoo. One day, a Doberman pup joined the animals in residence. He immediately caught Chiquita in his mouth and tossed her into the air. Apparently, he'd decided the expansive acreage was not large enough for two dogs. "She adapted to our family in moments," Lenny said. "She loves body warmth, obeys well, and is smart."

Golden retriever Chinoa's white fluff of a pom-pom tail, a grooming gift from the ever-smiling Maria

Jesus, grew from puppyhood to adulthood chained to a doghouse and a gate at the home of a night watchman. *Chinoa*, an indigenous word meaning "cloud," now roamed the fenced acres as the alpha dog, herding the menagerie away from the gate when visitors arrived (except for Barbara, who liked to escape). Later that evening, Chinoa welcomed me by reclining at the foot of my bed as if to ensure my safety for the night.

Estrella, pronounced "es-tray-ya" for "star" in Spanish, was a heartbreaker. Lenny and Joan found her scrawny body wobbling down their road, a wire wrapped around her neck. After removing the wire, they shooed her away. After all, they had five dogs already. Estrella persisted. Serpent-like, she wiggled under the front gate. The size of a stick of cotton candy with the lightness of a dandelion fluff, Estrella sat quietly one morning in the dewy grass. Next-door neighbor "Crazy Isaac" had been drinking the night before and awoke to find his garbage cans overturned. Blaming local dogs, he roared out into the yard with a nine-millimeter pistol. Unfortunately, the first dog he saw was Estrella in her own yard. His bullet shattered the bone in her front left leg. Estrella now walked with a limp and wiggly tail. "She's a ray of light," Lenny said. "She'll take a running leap into the air for sheer fun." She sat on my lap the first chance she got.

Tutu, named after Archbishop Desmond Tutu of South Africa, reigned as the only male of the canines.

A miniature schnauzer, Tutu, followed in the footsteps of Joan's previous schnauzer, Bo-Bo (named after Boutros Boutros-Ghali), who died a year earlier. Tutu, built solid like a muscular tank, wreaked havoc with all of the animals. He jumped at the young cats, Popcorn and Peanut, wrapping his mouth around their heads and dragging them across the kitchen floor. When he released them, the male Peanut attacked Tutu from the rear and started the game anew. I began to enjoy the chaos.

Lenny and Joan didn't believe in puppy school training for their charges. They blessed each animal with individual love and receive the same in return. I tried their technique with Barbara that first night. Barbara was attempting to mount my roommate's bed, her usual resting place. I walked over and said, "No, Barbara, not tonight. There are other places to sleep."

My tone surprised me. I stroked Barbara's head. She gazed up with liquid-black coffee eyes. She had to choose. Her new love or her old bed? She seemed to shrug her shoulders. A sigh heaved from her barrel chest, and she stepped down onto the hardwood floor, clacking her toenails over to my side of the room to lie at the foot of my bed. I fell in love at that moment.

The Ticos must be doing something right by their canine pets. An estimated one million abandoned dogs roam Costa Rican streets. With so much focus on exotic fauna such as scarlet and great green macaws, nesting turtles, and assorted migratory butterflies, dogs wisely blend in with the environment. At Amigos de las Aves and the Hatched to Fly Free program site in Alajuela, scientist Alan Taylor noted that since the stray dogs left at their doorstep had become part of the hatchery's family, macaw theft plummeted.

One evening, with the pups milling about rubbing against my legs, I accept a banana bit dropped into my hand by a fiery-billed aracari. Mating pairs of parrots resided in two cages on the patio that overlooked the landscaped chicken yard. Any one or more of the six cats slept intertwined amid the glassware on the shelves. The evening held the aura of Edward Hicks' painting, *Peaceable Kingdom*, depicting a lion lying down with a lamb and other assorted creatures in a tropical valley. I had stepped into the lush canvas.

I strolled with the dogs down to the river fence. Me alone with six dogs, chatting away about the day's events. Never would I have imagined such an evening. I had become a dog whisperer.

FACT: The current Intergovernmental Panel on Climate Change (IPCC) sees Costa Rica as a hotspot for changing weather conditions in the next fifty years. In the near-term, rainfall patterns and water levels vary from the ongoing effects of El Niño. Costa Rica is known primarily for its earthquakes, but a climate crisis-generated sea level rise will likely increase the frequency of tsunamis as well.

Tsunami

fincas guarded
with guns and gates

in a country
with no military

to keep rain and
floods at bay

Young Balinese dancers preserve their heritage through performances that are deeply felt and generously given.

Paradise Lost and Found

Bali

"Taksi! Taksi! Taksi!"

Faces glared, signs waved with words foreign and familiar: Wayan Ada. Smith-Barker. My first inhalation of Bali dragged in cigarette smoke, diesel oil, exhaust fumes. I held tight to my only certainty: the email printout stating, "Meet hotel driver at Starbucks."

Where was I? Covina, California? Zanesville, Ohio? The corner of 17th and Broadway, New York City? Just minutes ago, I had descended through a thick blanket of cumulus clouds toward Indonesia, the archipelago of multi-shaped islands dotting the ocean below. Now I stood on solid ground at the Denpasar Airport, Bali.

I towed my luggage over a faded orange carpet past stern customs agents. A haunting gauntlet of money-changers wagged their forms at all passersby. I seemed to have stepped into a remake of Fellini's *Satyricon*. At the terminal's entry, a hoard of bodies leaned into a rope, fanning signs marked with resort names, limousine services, guests to retrieve.

My expectations of a spiritual respite crashed and burned—fast. Once on the humid sun-drenched street, I wended my way past tall palms, traffic fumes and horns, and more shouts of "*taksi, taksi, taksi.*" Arms waved at me to buy this, buy that, proxy to the consumerism I had flown nearly 14,000 miles to escape. Did Bali want me here only to spur its economy? Was I wearing a sign, "Consumer, Ready to Shop"?

At the assigned Starbucks, I connected with my traveling companions. We promptly moved into the abrupt stop-and-go rush hour traffic of Denpasar. Dogs limped and stretched along the narrowing two-lane streets that seemed ordered only by a random traffic signal or two as we sped out of the city. Every other house resembled a temple, separated by languishing half-started structures. Bottles of petrol teetered on thin-legged tables close to the van as the driver swerved to avoid hordes of motorcyclists. I began to identify with Rangda, the Balinese black-faced child-eating demon, ready to chomp off one of these lovely smiling faces. There had to be more here. I exhaled.

"You need Bali," my daughter had said.

I thought so too. I needed Bali with its reputation of lilting landscapes and calm, smiling people as portrayed in a National Geographic video. I needed Bali to heal. Not the Hollywood version of healing—I didn't make it past page five of *Eat, Pray, Love*, nor did I consider wasting my time on the film. I'd been romantically involved with the island of Bali for over twenty years. As a rebel with a cause, I hung on the edge of American culture wanting something cleaner, more pristine as a way of living life. From afar and offshore, Bali seemed to offer a spiritual living situation. The Balinese say they have no art, they ARE art. They walk their talk daily, or so I had heard. I needed that. I hoped my visit to Bali would reveal some secret path that I could follow. Within the past ten years I'd lived through the death of a marriage, the death of both parents, the loss of a home in the downturned economy, the loss of my best-friend brother. Loss, loss, loss. Just before leaving for Bali, my siblings decided to sell the family homestead in Ohio that I had wanted to preserve.

Arriving at my Sayan area abode near the town of Ubud, my transition to the island still disjointed, I decided to seek healing and healers. I read much about Bali's healers, important facts such as "Americans should pay at least $10 for the healer." Some Balinese healers have their own websites these days. Offshore, Bali offered a new take on spiritual living. Decades ago, I dragged my three young children to hear Balinese Gamelan Sekar Jaya in Berkeley, California. I researched Balinese customs and reviewed Margaret Mead's works on their daily life.

My first intimate meeting with Balinese culture happened shortly after dropping my luggage at the hotel. Descending into the bowels of the Central Market in Ubud, the real Balinese beckoned from concrete floors, from food stalls. I watched vendors frying tofu triangles, filling a plastic bag (yes, they use plastic bags in Bali) with an orange-red oily sauce that shouted "pungent," tossing in the fried tofu then flipping and tying the bag. Everyone seemed to be waving their arms at me, beckoning me to check out their wares and buy something. A sinking feeling engulfed me. I wouldn't find fulfillment here on my spiritual quest away from the profane, the almighty dollar, the "we're supporting their economy" talk notwithstanding. I had to get away from the tourists, away from the Ubud Central Market, out of the clutches of Cost Plus on steroids.

Outside the market at the far end stood a temple. Women dressed in their green and gold skirts and sheer blouses lit incense, bent over square woven palm-leaf baskets filled with ritual offerings: flowers, seeds, a Ritz cracker on one. Sprinkling holy water over some offerings, they bowed to each and every manifestation of god.

A few days later I met Anom and Dayu. Anom (Ida Bagus Anom Surawar) is a master mask maker in the town of Mas. Dayu is his wife. Both had taken part in the Bali exhibit at the Asian Art Museum in San Francisco that I visited several times before my trip. Anom and Dayu were open and sharing, made a genuine connection with people, and both spoke excellent English.

Anom animatedly espoused art as a part of life. "Everything a person does, says, or writes is important. It becomes part of the visible life," the mask maker said, speaking of Sarasvati, goddess of creativity.

"Even my eternal lists and Post-it notes?"

"Yes, of course, what every writer has written is sacred."

Anom's views tugged at me, allowing a subtle letting go of the guilt about keeping so many books and papers. He explained why the Balinese make offerings daily out of honor for good and evil. The Balinese respect the demons as well as the gods and goddesses.

"We make offerings in thanks for the good we receive."

This contrasts to our Western culture and mono-theistic religions, where evil exists as something to over-come, something to beat down. The Balinese honor the demons, paying homage to the black witch Rangda as well as Rama and Sita.

Dayu was especially forthcoming about Balinese family life. She and Anom have three children. Accord-ing to Dayu, the reason every other compound looks like a temple is because it actually houses the family temple. Extended families stay together within these compounds to care for orphaned grandchildren, unmarried siblings, and aged artist parents who still have much to teach the next generation.

"Our seventeen-year-old son would turn off his cell phone when he sees I am calling."

Just as my son had done during his teen years.

Little by little the real Bali began to appear, to creep in. People relating to each other as fellow humans who happen to live on this earth. I told Dayu about the pressure of selling my parents compound, that one acre in rural Ohio that had fed us through the 1950s and 1960s. Then the Brahmin Dayu gave me a special gift.

"Here in Bali we would not sell the family compound," she said.

"How fortunate for you. I'm now the matriarch, so to speak, of my family, so I feel the loss of the land."

"In Bali we believe in the actual. To keep your family and the land with you always, collect a jar of dirt, the soil from your parents' land. The family home will be with you forever."

Now, why hadn't I thought of that? Brilliant. On return to the hotel, I would email Joanne and Web, my parents' Ohio neighbors, with this request, noting the urgency of this task since my siblings and I were closing the sale on the acre in just a few days.

Leaving the mask-maker's family compound, I thanked both Anom and Dayu for their visible and invisible gifts. Anom's gift, in addition to his mask of Ganesha, the loyal spirit of Rama, was his pronouncement that every word and note I'd written (even the grocery lists) were parts of the truth.

Later that night, we dined at Café Lotus with its mix of Western and Indonesian cuisine. We learned chefs clean and boil the salad ingredients to meet Western intestinal requirements. The Indonesian Bintang beer easily became a favorite among our group, since wine cost several times the American price. After the dinner, we were served the *Ramayana*, a production of the Hindu epic drama of Rama and his loyal but disparaged wife, Sita, accompanied by a female gamelan orchestra. This was the Bali I came to see. An all-female gamelan group save for the male drum leader. These women in fuchsia lace and gold costumes fiercely attacked their instruments, hammering madly at the accompaniment. The dance artistry moved eternal, the spirits of the Bali past, suspended, made real.

Continuing my search for the true Bali, the spiritual Bali, I arranged an interview the next day with Dr. Ketut Suardana, Master of Philosophy and Chairman of the Yayasan Mudra Swari Saraswati Foundation in Ubud. In addition, Dr. Suardana is the husband of restaurateur Janet De Neefe of Casa Luna in Ubud. Together with De Neefe, he founded the Ubud Writers & Readers Festival after the October 2002 bombings in the tourist district of Kuta on Bali.

Because of his interest in religion, I asked Dr. Suardana about the Balinese concept of good and evil. "How can the Balinese respect the demons as well as the gods and goddesses?"

Dr. Suardana explained that as Hindus, the Balinese consider each person, animal, plant and object to be a manifestation of "god" and there is no wrong attitude from any of these manifestations. They feel an obligation to the tourist, who confers prosperity onto the island and its people. He's completing his master's thesis on the theology of tourism and noted that the Balinese believe they should treat guests in their land as they would treat a god.

"We have three debts in our theology: to God, to holy men, and to our ancestors at our family shrines. It's a threefold theory of state, culture, and capital."

"But what about all the vendors thrusting their wares at tourists? Doesn't this confound your theology?"

"We see the massive materialism of the West and watch that it should not happen here. If materialism hits Bali, it will implode."

After the interview, returning to Sayan Terrace, the taxi driver told me of his two sons and one daughter who needed more money for school. He was tired of sending taxes to Jakarta and the corrupt Indonesian government. He had a brother who works as a bartender on a California cruise ship for eight months then returns to Bali for the remainder of the year.

"He makes big bucks, my brother. This helps the family."

I felt the world contracting, shrinking, as I stepped out of his taxi. Capitalism, the ugly beast, might be the next demon.

Jolting in yet another taxi to my apartment in San Francisco, I thought about what I had actually discovered in Bali. The Balinese I met spoke about their firmly held truths: Keep things in balance. Good and evil go hand in hand, so respect the bad in your life. Family is most important, and so is giving.

This current American taxi driver, with newsboy hat pulled down over his brow, interrupted my thoughts. "We need more tourism here!" he kvetched. "We should make Treasure Island into Disneyland North. We should do everything we can to attract more tourists! We need more business to boost our local economy."

"Let's convert Treasure Island in San Francisco Bay into a Bali theme park, where inhabitants zip around on motor scooters—with women dressed in lacy greens and golds and men spruced up in the sarong-esque *kamben* and striking *udengs*; where sacrifices of baskets, flowers and nuts greet the visitors as they step on the sidewalks and inhale incense and peace; where the concrete remains of a navy station are turned into lush, verdant rice paddies and tourists can meander for hours on end resting their hearts," I suggested.

"Naw, I don't think that would be a draw," he replied.

I waved to the driver as he sped down my dimly lit street. Demons of tourism floated over his cab, as it turned left, then disappeared. I blessed those demons and bowed to the good spirits of sharing and giving. Unlocking the front door, I gathered up a brown box left by the postal service. It contained the jar of soil, tiny pale-brown pebbles from my parents' Ohio acre.

I placed it next to their wedding photograph, lit a candle in blessing, and bowed in *namaste*.

FACT: In recent years, the paradise of Bali has unraveled. Home to this year's G20 president, Indonesia must now work to reduce its greenhouse gas emissions by forty-one percent with international assistance by 2030. Who will step up to put the brakes on temperature changes and the accompanying sea level rise that will destroy tourist beaches and family homes in the coastal areas? Kuta Beach is now being rebuilt through a public-private partnership.

Unraveled

rusted motorbikes
balance entire families
across gas-fumed streets

meditative rice terraces
frazzled greenhouse gasses

end effect
Kuta Beach
needs a facelift

Sigiriya in Sri Lanka: it was a wonder to climb. Nearly straight up on zigzagging metal stairs, high humidity adds to the challenge.

Eighth Wonder
of the World

Sri Lanka

"Well, is it? Is Sigiriya the Eighth Wonder of the World?" I detected a hint of cynicism, mixed with a whisper of pride, in Shirly Fernando's question. I dripped and drooped from the six-hundred-foot descent. The temperature registered a mere 86 degrees Fahrenheit, but the 93 percent humidity on this well-turned-out, bright-sky January day in central Sri Lanka sucked my climbing energy and goodwill.

Shirly Fernando—Shirly is a man's name in Sri Lanka—served as my guide throughout this seren- dipitous journey through Old Ceylon. I'd "won" a plane ticket to Sri Lanka—an exciting bit of luck until I learned that my prize covered only half the distance to the teardrop-shaped island off the southeast tip of India. The plane ticket covered London—Colombo— London. I lived in San Francisco, nine flight hours from my port of departure.

Serendipity: the act of making fortunate dis- coveries by accident. Horace Walpole created the word "serendipity" from an ancient name for Sri Lanka, *Serendip*. Out of a glass bowl on a California winter afternoon, my business card had pulled up a supreme act of serendipity. The precious London—Colombo—London round-trip ticket (airport taxes not included) had to be used in one year. I started to sweat the trip immediately. Collecting the ticket proved a challenge. Outside the U.S. and European Union, things move tortuously. A simple process such as purchasing an airline ticket with a SriLankan Airlines voucher called for patience, fortitude, and daily phone calls to New York and Colombo. The extra challenge of getting to London (airport taxes not included) to connect up with the SriLankan Airlines flight proved the easy part.

Once I landed in Sri Lanka's capital of Colombo, my three-week tour took off with the assigned Shirly Fernando driving with focused extreme care. After one week of driving north, we headed inland to Sigiriya, a contender for the title of eighth wonder of the world. Or so Shirly claimed.

The previous day and night, "unseasonal" (a commonly used word these days due to climate change) monsoon-like rains drenched the grounds of the Kashyapa Lions Rock Inn, my pre-Sigiriya rest stop. From the open-air patio of the Kashyapa Lions Rock, I surveyed the stone wonder of Sigiriya from several miles away. It loomed determinedly out of the verdant chaparral and low trees, jutting high and alone out of the landscape. An evening walk up the muddy, flooded red dirt road bordering the inn revealed a shadowed, reddish-beige mountain island, beckoning across the scrub-bush-covered plain. Sigiriya—shaped like a hardened loaf of bread, its top full of outcropped dripping trees and greenery, slashes of black rock, and gouges from waterfalls—stood majestic. The morning ride over the rutted main road to the main gate of Sigiriya rocked the Nissan Bluebird Sylphy. I sat in the front seat to avoid motion sickness.

Shirly, of course, embellished and enthused over Sigiriya's history. The rock, a UNESCO World Heritage Site, is the ruins of a palace of King Kashyapa I (or Kassapa I) (448-495 CE). This king's brief reign began under evil portent. Kashyapa I assassinated his father, Dhatusena, in a most heinous manner. Clearly, my guide did not think highly of King K: "How do you like that! Kashyapa walled his own father into the palace bulwark for a slow death!"

Dhatusena, Kashyapa's father, builder of many *wewas* or tank reservoirs that remain functional today, had ruled with respect from the ancient nerve center of Anuradhapura for many decades. Kashyapa I's younger brother, Moggallana—reading the tea leaves—fled to India, where he bided his time.

Kashyapa ventured out to build the Sigiriya (Lion Rock) fortress above the forests. Now a major tourist attraction, he embedded fresco galleries of buxom painted ladies thought to depict Tara the Mahayana goddess, worshiped as the great savior. He erected staircases cascading out of a lion's mouth and between its giant paws. The Sigiriya of the twenty-first century I met that January day still hosted the twenty-one "Maidens of the Clouds," many preserved in splendid colors in an overhang gallery out of the elements.

"Let's begin the ascent," Shirly coaxed us after we ambled through the ruins and grounds, coated in naturally shorn green grass. Cows with their one or two calves grazed among the raised walls that once housed King Kashyapa's workers.

A pilgrimage to the gallery of naked goddesses raised my heart rate instantaneously. The climb to the top of the six-hundred-foot Sigiriya by way of pinging wrought-iron stairs should have been easy for a runner like me. I neglected, however, to consider this ascent as the equivalent of marching straight up sixty flights of stairs in a skyscraper. In high heat and humidity. Without stopping.

The iron stairs to the goddess gallery were bolted into the rock itself. Cakes of rust encircled the bolts. Some caged steps, supposedly there to prevent accidental falls, did not inspire confidence. Of course, the rusted bolts precariously keeping the stairs adjoined to the mountain screamed for my attention. My heart raced. I closed my eyes to avoid thoughts, dizziness, and the prospect of a fatal event—the equivalent of crossing my fingers to avoid tumbling down the three-hundred-foot sheer cliff. Visions of the entire mesh-enclosed stairwell tumbling over the edge, bouncing off Lion

Rock, slowed time. If I closed my eyes, I would not see it coming. The bolts held, to my surprise. I panted at the gallery.

The Sri Lankan damsels continue to inspire Sinhalese graffiti and poems on any surface reachable, with rich reds and golds haloing their exotic beauty. The panicked climb was worth it. Sexy murals indeed.

King Kashyapa patronized the Buddhist monks living at Sigiriya at the time. They'd built a vast city of grottos, ponds, cisterns, and rock gardens both at ground level and up to the terraced top of Lion Rock. The rock palace forming Sigiriya's core was impregnable.

Again, Shirly editorialized on the king's brief history. Kashyapa, hearing of Moggallana's return from India in 495 CE, descended from the fortress to crush his brother. Encountering a bog while atop his elephant, Kashyapa became isolated from his fleeing army.

"Kashyapa did not have the loyalty of his army. They left him!" Shirly approved of this development. Seeing that he would be captured, Kashyapa "fell on his sword," said guide Fernando, cheering this outcome. Upon Kashyapa's death, Moggallana returned Sigiriya to the Mahayanist Buddhist monks who previously inhabited the site, thus ensuring the preservation of some of its splendor.

We next passed through the Cloud Maidens gallery, paying homage to the rich greens, reds, and ochers, which have held their mystique despite the monsoon of time. Past leaning boulders demarking the site's entry, I strode upward. I considered myself in good physical condition. After all, I was running at least three or four half-marathons a year. San Francisco may have its hills but they're not quite this steep. The direct ascent up six hundred vertical feet from the surrounding grounds would challenge any visitor's cardio health. Did I mention it was hot and humid?

Emptying two water bottles and soaking my nylon backpack all the way through, I willed myself up the stairs past two barefoot workers polishing the metal mirror wall with steel scrubbers the size of tooth-brushes. Reaching the nest-level landing at the lion's paws, I sat staring into space, soon filled with a club of macaques frolicking on the palace walls.

At this point, Guide Shirly elected to leave me to ascend to the top alone.

"I've done it for thirty years, every time I guide tourists here. I have seen the top; it has not changed." Shirly reclined in the shade, chatting with colleagues on the first landing after the initial climb through the naked maiden murals.

Alone with tourists from Britain, Australia, Russia, France, Sri Lanka, and the forest's resident monkeys, I clung to a rickety metal rail up slanted steel steps. We squeezed past each other on the very narrow stairs.

Once at the top, palace gardens—overgrown and displaying bulwark designs—led to a large stone seat signed "The Throne." Some records verify it as the monks' bench, placed there to take in the surrounding view. The throne label did not apply, though, as the stone seat most likely was where a teacher would instruct fellow monks or novices in Buddhist practices and readings.

Sitting under a bodhi tree sprouting out of the ruins, I watched the east-facing mountains change colors and located my hotel, far off among deep-green shrub trees. The cooling breeze played over the top landing. I imagined monks living here year-round, just sitting on top of the rock, enjoying the zephyrs for weeks on end. I watched a monarch-like butterfly softly open and close its wings.

On the descent, again slowly due to the slippery metal stairs, I returned to Shirly's challenge, his question. Many world sites have earned the label of Eighth Wonder of the World and are duly recognized. Natural formations. Pre-1900 creations. Post-1900 manifestations. Only one person has achieved fame as a "wonder of the world." That would be André the Giant (1946-1993). André was a French-born professional wrestler and actor. Never heard of him? Neither had I.

Sigiriya falls in the pre-1900 category of world wonders, competing with the likes of the Statue of Liberty, the Brooklyn Bridge, Machu Picchu (Peru), the Taj Mahal (India), Angkor Wat (Cambodia), the moai statues of Easter Island (Chile), and the Great Wall of China. From my perch atop the rock with its panoramic view of open sky, rainforests, and the Knuckles Mountains, Sigiriya definitely tops the two United States entries. I've dined on pizza and ice cream beneath the Brooklyn Bridge on such a sunny afternoon and climbed to the top of the torch of Miss Liberty. The Great Wall of China, visited in 1995 with my two young daughters, is long and continuous. Yet, compared to these three contenders, I felt that Sigiriya deserved the honor. Building a city high up in the heavens—hauling all the accouterments of daily life into the clouds—gave me a new appreciation of the vision of this king. I had difficulty just moving my one body and damp daypack to the top of the plateau.

"Well, what do you say? Is Sigiriya the eighth wonder of the world?" Shirly waited with pride, as well as a touch of sarcasm gurgling below the question's surface. I hadn't the heart to tell him I'd never visited any of the big-time Seven Wonders of the known world and had nothing with which to compare.

"Yes, definitely, Sigiriya would win my vote for now." Shirly Fernando had done his day's work. He beamed and softly waggled his head.

FACT: Recent upheavals in Colombo summon thoughts of Shirly Fernando, travel guide turned friend. The pandemic disrupted the country's most important industries, especially tourism.

Then government mismanagement led to food and fuel shortages. The climate crisis threatens Sri Lanka's groundwater and drinking water. One of the hottest countries in the world, Sri Lanka faces crop failures and food insecurity.

Rising waters

to weather this storm
dear friend
hold your family tight

keep your faith in us
   may holy waters
      bless your every day

Shaman Juan Chiyal Queju readies the room for my ceremonial visit. "Your life will change today," said Shaman Juan.

Mayan Shaman:
Your Life Will Change

Guatamala

I recognize in you my other I.

—Mayan proverb

I was in a darkened open room, candlelit—the tall votive kind—with a myriad of saints gazing down at me from a wooden shelf. The Mayans blend the Catholic Madonna with Maximón (pronounced "Ma-shi-mon"), a pre-Columbian Mayan god of the underworld also known as Mam or Grandfather, an effigy of which stands on the concrete floor, draped in a blue-and-golden robe. Cups of multicolored wildflowers and strewn metal pots line the turquoise- and green-painted back wall, hung with photos of the shaman's Mayan community. The scent of burning beeswax and chicken feed float through the air. A graceful chorus of fresh-picked flowers litter the painted floor where I sit and later would kneel. Hens cluck outside in the narrow passageway, cluttered with plastic containers, colorful tinsel bags, and old coffee tins, through which I'd just squeezed to enter the shaman's chamber.

Juan Chiyal Queju, a Tz'utujil Maya shaman from Santiago di Atitlán, beams at me as I stumble in. Immediately I knew him. He is my size, clad in white pants with red vertical stripes tied with a multicolored sash. A billowing ruby shirt with deep blue stripes covers his upper torso, a rouge-blue scarf envelopes his head. Open-toed huaraches caress his wide feet.

After I enter, Shaman Juan tells me his name, "Chiyal," means "obsidian" in Mayan. I reply that obsidian is one of my favorite stones—an igneous rock, a natural glass, silica-rich and formed by the rapid cooling of viscous volcanic lava. It is known as a protective stone that shields against negative energy.

His eyes say he has guided many to know themselves at the shores of Lake Atitlán, which lies nestled amid three volcanoes.

No hablo español muy bien. I mumble my go-to phrase while traveling in South America. Not that I would comprehend Juan's Tz'utujil dialect. But in my memory of the morning spent with him, we did speak directly to each other. Somehow. It could have been my mind and soul entered another space with his soul, and we communicated with interlacing brain waves. I'd been an avid reader of Carlos Castaneda's *The Teachings of Don Juan: A Yaqui Way of Knowledge* decades earlier.

Dolores, my guide, sat in the chamber with us.

She was to serve as translator of the ritual. Perhaps I would hand Dolores the three hundred quetzals—two hundred Qs for her to translate and the remainder to Juan to work his magic.

In Mayan cosmology, the universe continues in its creation through mutual divine-human interaction. Humans practice sympathetic magic. All things mirror each other; we imitate events in Dream Time. The highest cultivation of Mayan spiritual practice is the deepening of the soul. A Mayan shaman attends a person's *chu'el* or holistic harmony. One's state may be imbalanced because of internal or external dynamics that affect a person's wholeness. It can manifest in spiritual, mental, emotional, or/and physical ailments.

Why was I there, in that room at that moment in time? Ostensibly, I was attending a writing workshop in Guatemala. I'd always been drawn by the Guatemalan colors—red, gold, black, brown—the very Mayan spirit interwoven in their fabrics and their lives, as a culture, a nation, an indigenous people.

Why did I seek out a shaman to understand my life back in the States? My children were launched. The youngest, my son, had completed college three years before. He was living in Boston at the time. I had a grandson in San Diego. My middle child was evolving somewhere. Then a thought entered my mind, where was I going.

Shaman Juan began the Mayan initiation ceremony to unlock my authentic powers. Something I've searched for since the age of five. I knew I had such powers but how to unlock them, set them free into the atmosphere? His voice hummed deep and sonorous. He whirred, droned. His was a vivid, kind voice. I was not afraid. This was most important to me—to find my authentic self, whatever that meant, as if I was looking for an igneous sunrise.

Who was this person—my self, the real me? I had been searching for this self for more than sixty years. I'd try any path to find it. Visiting a shaman made total sense. I always claimed I'd try most anything once. I wanted to change; I didn't want to stay locked in my old quiet body, not speaking to anyone. I didn't want to stay in hiding. I didn't want to trip numbly through life. I wanted to speak my truth. I wanted to see how far I could push myself to open my heart to see what was inside. And what to let in.

Juan Chiyal blended Mayan-Catholic rituals of spirituality six thousand feet up in the mountains above Lago de Atitlán. He immediately claimed my Mayan spirit was the feathered serpent who flies across the heavens between the sun and stars. I felt it, the arc across the black night. He said he would teach me to honor my *k'an* (snake) spirit to open up my life.

Juan continued the ceremony. In his muted voice, he chanted much like a priest at a Catholic mass. Juan then lit a host of skinny red, gold, green, and azure candles spread out on the floor in front of me. The blossoms carpeting the floor seemed important. He promised to teach me to pray to my *k'an*, my Mayan feathered serpent. How did I know this? I didn't hear English words come out of his or Dolores' mouth. She remained nearby, like an archangel hovering above my shoulder. Juan said I was *k'an*, the feathered serpent. He didn't say I was the guarded jaguar, ferocious and strong. He didn't say I was Hunab Ku, the Mayan creator god.

I felt my Mayan spirit, the *k'an* or Kukulkan, the plumed serpent festooned with the feather of a quetzal. I'm to shed my skin as I cross the heavens in the path of the sun and stars transversing the sky. My spirit brokers peaceful trade and good communications with other creatures. My *k'an* continues in renewal and rebirth. Good housekeeping habits I've always had.

As I left Juan Chiyal's ceremonial room, he grinned at me and said, "Your life will change today." I comprehended his Tz'utujil phrases. I nodded, though most likely I heard Dolores's whispered English. Or did I actually understand Juan's voice and words in another sphere of consciousness?

Being blessed in early morning candlelight in a flower-petal-strewn prayer ceremony and asking the blessings of Grandfather Sky and Grandmother Earth opened a vital hole in my chest for the world to enter and for me to fly out. The dry dust caused my tongue to stick to the bottom of my mouth. *Was this the taste of fear or of freedom?* This thought walked across the floor of my mind. My brain waves seemed to hover, to stand still for once. I sensed a deep connection with all beings, all humans and other animals and birds who shared life each day high above a lake that gave them sustenance for their bodies and their souls.

FACT: Shaman Juan told me, "Your life will change." This now has become the mantra for the earth as every day brings new climate crisis challenges we must weather. Unfortunately, the global poor will experience more effects of the climate crisis than wealthier countries. Guatemala has suffered extreme weather events, hurricanes, erratic weather patterns (spikes and drops in temperature), torrential rains, drought, and unexpected frost.

Metamorphosis

your life will change
    Shaman Juan
    wisdom

weathering the change
    now calls for us
    to transform into we

metamorphosis
    on becoming the feathered
    serpent searing the sky

to enjoin all together
moving in one long arc
    oh this planet

In Moulay Idriss we heard singing in the darkened passages. We stood outside the open door, then were invited in to share in the fortieth day after death celebration by the deceased's family and friends.

An Open Door

Morocco

In the house of lovers, the music never stops,
the walls are made of songs and the floor dances.

—Rumi

I packed for my Morocco journey reminding myself: *open mind, open mind.*

I hadn't visited a Muslim country since teaching English in Turkey in the early 1970s. At that time, Istanbul—and much of the country outside of that "Paris of the Orient"—functioned as a secular republic. Yes, the *azan* or call to prayer summoned Muslims five times each day. The *muezzin*'s tenor intoned the reminder from the mosque's minaret, or—a sign of the times—from a tape recorder through the loudspeaker atop the spindly tower. Apart from these rituals, Turkish people included non-Muslims and foreigners in their daily lives. Attending the wedding of a fellow Turkish teacher's widowed mother, I felt the family warmly wrap me into their celebration.

The world changed drastically over the four ensuing decades. The events of September 11, 2001, two brutal American-led Iraq wars, the war in Afghanistan, strife exploding throughout the Middle East, suspicion and persecution of Muslims in America, unbalanced reporting by U.S. corporate media—all jelled to rattle my traveler's psyche.

Women's status in Morocco had seen some progress. A movement had sprung from fomenting social and political upheavals. Morocco's path merged into the Arab Spring that shook so many Middle Eastern countries. Morocco transitioned from an authoritarian monarchy to a "progressive" (caution: words are relative) king. In this sociopolitical cauldron, women's rights floated out into open public discourse. Women in Morocco gained legal rights within the family but not full integration into the public arena. As one protester aptly said, "This is a critical time. There are two steps in a revolution: You break it, and then you build something new. That's the hardest."

Indeed, my travels throughout the planet tended to break some beliefs and prejudices. Building something new in their place challenged reality.

Morocco—the word itself spills out into a mix of aromatic spices, geometric arrays of raging colors, graceful Arabic characters, words like *djellabas*, those multicolored unisex robes, and *hijabs*—veils hiding a woman's head and neck. Once my plane had touched down and I entered the city, the beehive frenzy that is

Fez invaded my senses. The medina, that old walled city of narrow passages, seized my entire body, churned my conscious mind, and overwhelmed me. Zigzags of steep steps puzzled, riots of color and shapes dazzled, yeasty round bread slammed each inhale. Under circling bees, sweet honeyed nougat tempted, and *ras al hanout*, that eternal blend of spices—nutmeg, coriander, cumin, ginger, turmeric, cinnamon, paprika, black pepper, cardamom, allspice, and cloves tempered with a dash of salt—shouted: *Morocco, you have arrived!*

Fez, once Morocco's capital and still its cultural center, jangled and surprised. Most inhabitants speak Arabic and French; visitors are often greeted with a "*Bonjour, Madame. Bonjour, Monsieur.*" The air inside this World Heritage Site caressed my face like an evocative touch from a beloved *habibi*, a frequently repeated term in Moroccan and Arabic poetry.

The familiar call to prayer of the *muezzin* comforted me, calming the frenetic life within the city walls. On an evening at *Riad Zany*, the restored permanent home of Australians Suzanna Clark and Sandy McCutcheon, we stood on the roof patio while the labyrinth of Fez oozed in all directions. At sunset, *muezzin* voices lifted in praise to Allah, the singing reverberating in all directions. The sound enveloped and levitated me above the concrete floor. Swirling in a slow circle, eyes closed, I joined the unseen callers in a sort of prayer.

After a few days of equilibration to Fez, I traveled

to Moulay Idriss Zerhoun, the sacred city—another medina, much smaller than Fez, yet holy to the people of Morocco. Within walking distance of Volubilis, the well-preserved Roman ruins, Moulay Idriss drapes over several knolls at the base of Mount Zerhoun. In the eighth century, Moulay Idriss I arrived, intermarrying within local Berber tribes. He then introduced Islam to Morocco and established a four-century ruling dynasty.

The sacred heart of Morocco and a pilgrimage destination during the full month of fasting of Ramadan, Moulay Idriss only recently opened to foreign visitors. Entry into the guesthouses of the hilly medina requires a special local taxi service: donkeys. Drivers loaded and roped my bag onto one of their animals. The kindly creature then clomped steadily up steep stairs, picking its hooves over cobblestone alleyways to Riad Dar Zerhoune. Hajiba, the guesthouse manager, in the excellent English she learned in elementary school, said, "This is your home while you are here. I will help you."

Hiking around Moulay Idriss's outer perimeter on a sunny March day, voluptuous streams cascaded down the mountain and past the town's "swimming pool," a slab of pale gray concrete set near a side crop of the splashing waters. Women and children collected water from the numerous spouts of neighborhood fountains located throughout the city. One jolly woman motioned how strong she was and laughingly posed for my camera. Beaming, she hoisted two large plastic buckets and headed homeward.

In the evening, we visited Scorpion House (Dar Akrab) for dinner. Scorpion House serves as the personal retreat for Brit Mike Richardson, the proprietor of Café Clock in Fez. His terraced home afforded a spectacular view of Moulay Idriss, the green-tiled roof of the mosque, *tagine* and *brochette* stalls, and sunsets. Views extended out over the pale and painted homes of the town, stretching toward the undulating countryside and the Volubilis ruins.

After dining with Mike's guests and reveling in evening readings of poetry and prose, several of us descended into the medina to our *riad*, Dar Zerhoune. The sky, or what little we could see of it, was black, the time nearing eleven o'clock. Tunnels in the medina stood dark, sparingly lit by single bulbs hanging about at random. As we stumbled into one steep alleyway, we collectively stopped—singing greeted us. The voices soared. We halted outside an open door; a young woman and man beckoned us—a group of ten foreigners—to enter. In the center of a room, under wooden pillars, sat eight men. Sufis in their white gowns—*tennures*, a symbol of death—were rocking and singing, their faces ablaze with smiles of joy. Three held microphones. The tallest wore bright yellow pointy shoes. Another cradled his young son, feeding the boy a cookie. Women, children, and other men populated the surrounding audience. All present sang and rocked.

The ushers quickly seated us, carrying in extra

chairs. Young girls appeared with glasses of sweet mint tea and a tray of almond cookies. Attendees nodded in welcome as if we were expected neighbors. The Sufi choir's chanting rose to a boisterous pitch. The only Arabic word I understood—"Allah, Allah, Allah"—thrust against the rafters. The full force of their rhythm compelled my body to rock, to feel fully alive and transcendent. Time stopped.

After what seemed like an eternity, we rose, bowed our gratitude, and returned to our respective riads. I sat on my cot long into the night, quiet, meditative, and transformed.

The next morning, I met Magit, our Moulay Idriss guide. He beamed, exclaiming we'd experienced a "one-in-a-thousand event." We'd participated in the fortieth-day-after-death celebration, the end of the mourning period for a member of their community. That they had invited us in and extended a gracious welcome astounded and pleased him.

"If this would happen more often, we could learn from each other." Magit gazed out over the city's walls.

On my farewell to Moulay Idriss the next morning, I strolled through the town's central square just after sunrise. The tall Sufi from the past evening walked toward me, still resplendent in a white *djellaba*, a glowing *sikke* hat, and those remarkable bright yellow shoes. He sang still, a blissful smile on his face. As he passed, I again felt lifted off the ground by his joy and song. Greeting the morning with praise for the new day, his happiness swept over me.

122

My son once told me, when studying world religions in high school, the only creed that attracted him was Sufism. Now a jazz musician, he may have understood religion and the world better than I. When I close my eyes and "hear" that Sufi choir in full voice, my body still rocks and sways, again elevated and transported back to that room at midnight in Moulay Idriss, sharing moments with fellow beings. A celebration of death melded into a transformation of life. Open mind transmuted into open heart.

As the ancient Sufi saying teaches: "Some doors are only opened from inside."

FACT: Morocco will experience a ten- to twenty-percent decline in rainfall, with the most severe shortages affecting the Sahara. Wildlife elimination threatens extinction for mammals and birds. Nearly two hundred plant species, too, will disappear. Yet, Morocco built the Noor Ouarzazate power station, the world's largest concentrated solar power plant in the Sahara. An enormous array of curved mirrors distributed over nearly twelve square miles concentrate the sun's rays to generate electricity to share with its own and other peoples.

Eternity

Singing filled the night

fortieth day after death
celebrants linger
inviting strangers

cobblestones wet with rain
mirrors of the desert
free to all souls

all blessed

My father, Joe Pramik, worked underground in Ohio coal mines for decades. He enjoyed solving mechanical problems, but his real passion was planting and growing a vegetable garden.

Coal: Black to Gray and Back

England

The scent of machine oil caught at the back of my throat. Late-afternoon light hung throughout the vacant Geevor Mine's tin washing room. A solitary fly buzzed in the yawning October air. The sharp smell of spent black grease brought up a vision of my father in our frigid basement unraveling his body from lubricant-immersed coveralls. Bent over and weary, muscles knotted from ten to twelve hours in the mine, he'd peel off the black-and-gray-striped work clothes and toss them directly into the Double Dexter washing machine. His body sweat mixed with machine oil. The intermingling of these two smells identified my father during my early years in rural Ohio.

My thoughts raced in sync with the rumbling and rocking of the second-class railcar thumping me to St. Ives and the Geevor Tin Mine in Cornwall, that western finger of England poking into the Atlantic. Riotous British graffiti danced on passing empty coal cars. The syncopated clatter of the train and the image of the vacant railcars sparked memories of my coal miner father down in the tunnels below the earth's surface. The Cornwall guide noted that visitors could go underground into the Geevor Mine. This cinched my visit: I had always wanted to know how and what my father felt in the bowels of the earth. He was a quiet man, not given to embellishments, favoring one- or two-word answers. I wanted to feel what he felt in the blackness.

The Wheal Mexico, Geevor Mine's main dig, is estimated to be two hundred fifty years old. It operated as a tin-producing site until 1990, when the element's price crashed, rendering the operation unprofitable. At that time, the mine linked eighty-five miles of twisting tunnels, requiring on average a million gallons of water siphoned out daily. Black tin still rests under the Geevor surface, too costly to remove. The Geevor Mine now functions as a tourist venue. The land encircling the refurbished mine buildings stands bare, pocked with random chaparral ending at the Atlantic bluffs.

Descending into today's Geevor mineshaft required little courage on my part. The smooth, well-designed path alleviated any chance of my slipping or falling into a shaft. It almost seemed like a visit to Disneyland, but with the Atlantic Ocean crashing off the cliffs.

I donned a burgundy-colored laboratory coat and yellow hardhat to tour the Wheal Mexico. In the fully operating mine, the Geevor worker would descend via sets of long wooden ladders three hundred and fifty to five hundred feet below the surface. However, I stepped through a passageway that dropped only ninety feet underground. Once inside the two-foot-wide shaft, my eyes quickly adjusted to minimal light. I had to crouch only slightly in the short tunnel. The average height of the Cornish miner was recorded at five feet, two inches. My height.

Mine owners and the miners themselves considered it unlucky for women to enter the shafts. Females worked above ground. Known as bal maidens or bal maids, they smashed rock chunks into fragments and sorted ore from rocks by hand. Boys as young as five years old labored in the mine though. Ten-year-olds loaded rocks into kibbles or large buckets, while fourteen-year-olds, considered grown men, could detonate gunpowder. My father started his coal mining life at age fourteen, leaving high school as commanded by his strict father. This memory hit me full force in the dim light and saddened me as it always did. My father had placed first in a statewide test. Not attending high school created a huge hole in his life.

In the Geevor shaft, I ran my hand across the cold damp wall. I must remember to thoroughly scrub my hands because of the arsenic lacing the rock shaft, I reminded myself. Miners ate below during their workday rather than climb hundreds of feet up wooden ladders to the surface. Squatting in a tiny cutout room, two men would grasp their meat pie, called a pasty, by the crust's thickened end. They would discard this edge to avoid arsenic poisoning.

Tin mining required the men to work looking upward to hammer out the ore. They'd slither sideways through narrow shafts. The average life expectancy during the 1800s for a Cornish miner was twenty-four years. Accidents were frequent and numerous. In *Hazards & Heroes in Cornish Mines* by Allen Buckley, I'd read of teenager Jack Jarvis who stepped onto loose rock and plummeted seven meters into a stope (ore dig-out). According to Buckley, "Jack lay there, fully conscious but with a large piece of rock embedded in his skull and his legs and lower body buried by the rocks which had fallen with him." After extensive effort, fellow miners hauled him out, and he returned to the mine six months later with a dent in his head that lasted his lifetime. Cornwall miners, young and old, faced death by gassing with carbon monoxide, explosions from gunpowder and later dynamite, or sudden flooding of the entire shaft as storms pounded the sea against the tunneled cliffs.

Standing hunched in the black shaft lit by tiny bulbs, I thought of Jack Jarvis and tasted the dust hanging in the damp. Cornish men had eaten this dust daily. So had Ohio miners. In March 1940, dust from an extreme explosion of methane gas devastated the Willow Grove Mine, five miles from my rural Ohio home. Of one hundred eighty workers in the mine at that time, seventy-three died. Madeline Kanopsic, our longtime next-door neighbor, lost her husband Albert at age thirty-three that day. Pregnant with their first child, Madeline could never recall how she survived the ensuing months.

The Willow Grove Mine, owned by Hanna Coal Company, my father's employer, boasted that this "non-gaseous" mine was state of the art. Five years earlier, First Lady Eleanor Roosevelt had toured its two miles of underground shafts. After the explosion of black powder and invisible methane gas with a force that tore hinges off steel doors and split girders as if they were matchsticks, all mines were deemed gaseous. But seventy-three men lost their lives before mine owners admitted the constant danger.

Like their Cornish counterparts in tin mine disasters, Mine Superintendent John Richards and Outside Tipple Foreman Howard Sanders raced into the Willow Grove Mine to rescue their coworkers. Several men dragged out comatose miners and revived them. However, Richards and Sanders searched farther into the tunnels. They collapsed, dying from the afterdamp—unseen carbon monoxide gas. Twenty-three men survived the Willow Grove blast by losing consciousness on their three-mile journey to the mine's entrance. Their faces lay on the ground near the "good air."

Emerging from the Geevor shaft, I inhaled swiftly and deeply, unaware I'd held my breath while inside. I gasped, too, for the generations of Cornish men and boys who readied themselves each day for death, much like the Polish and Slavic miners did in eastern Ohio.

As writer Daphne du Maurier observed in *Vanishing Cornwall*, "Superstition flows in the blood of all three peoples." Though she meant the Cornish, Bretons, and

Irish, she might well have included the Polish Americans I know. Du Maurier continued, "Rocks and stones, hills and valleys, bear the imprint of men who long ago buried their dead beneath great chambered tombs and worshipped the earth goddess."

My father, working in eastern Ohio's black tunnels as did his forebears in southern Poland's underground labyrinths, wore scapular medals—amulets of sorts—to the Black Madonna, the Lady of Czestochowa, and other saints for protection from cave-ins, injuries, and death. Methodism guided Cornish miners, while Catholicism brought the balm of community to my hometown.

Du Maurier might well have described my father when she wrote: "There is in the Cornish character, smoldering beneath the surface, ever ready to ignite, a fiery independence, a stubborn pride." An early member of the United Mine Workers of America, my father was as stubborn as any Cornishman, laboring a long shift underground only to come home to hoe his quarter-acre garden in the summer dusk. And he walked the picket line when forced to strike against unsafe and unfair labor practices.

He made his livelihood and cared for his five children by plunging into the underground daily. He left home at eleven o'clock at night on the midnight shift, his biorhythms askew and inverted. The Cornish miners felt the same as they left the sunshine to their families above ground. In his waning years, my father recalled with crystal clarity his days down in the bowels of the earth. "It was cool, and quiet. You could do your work in silence. You'd hear only the hammer hitting the coal and rocks."

Yet for him, like for all miners, the specter of death was always present. His Polish ancestors never wished for a quick death. They would pray, "From pestilence, famine, fire, war, and sudden, unexpected death, preserve us, O Lord." The worst to happen was to meet death unprepared—away from home, lacking funds for a proper burial, or in a state of sin.

As I climbed out of the Geevor mine, I thought of the Bible that served both the Cornish miners and my father's people. The passage that reads *from dust we came and to dust we shall return.* Coal dust. Tin dust. Black or gray, much the same. My mouth felt stuffed with cotton balls.

The Atlantic heaved and crashed against the boulders below. Sea air and sunshine brightened the late afternoon. I half expected men and boys to pour out of the Geevor shafts and machine rooms, headed home to their families and a sturdy supper.

My first venture into Cornwall had brought to the surface neglected memories long submerged. The whiff of machine oil, the creak of a crank, dimness at ninety feet underground brought me to my father's world. His work in the mines sustained him and his family.

My father has been permanently underground for seven years now. What would he think about today's move away from coal, about the push to leave all fossil fuels underground? Or about his daughter signing every petition to keep coal locked below the earth's surface? I now understand that mining—ripping open the earth's innards to release carbon, fuel homes, adjust economies, and enrich the uber-wealthy—assures and guarantees the destruction of the planet.

Verdant fields encircled the Geevor site, adding to the poignancy of the moment. I gulped in the fresh sea air. And felt my father standing beside me, surveying the landscape with his approving crooked smile.

FACT: I grew up in Ohio coal country. I left the state for a healthier, cleaner environment in California. When I returned to Ohio for my children to visit their grandparents, my daughter would develop conjunctivitis from coal furnace exhaust. Wealthy nations have a responsibility to help poorer countries keep fossil fuels in the ground. Enough said.

Labyrinth

everywhere
everywhere
    enough said
a labyrinth
a honeycomb
tunnels underground
    cross each other
    waiting for the planet's
      c
       o
        l
           l
       a
            p
          s
      e

The *USS Hornet*—a battleship full of ghosts and ghost stories.

Ghost Ship: *USS Hornet* Conducts Spook Maneuvers

California

Darkness hangs opaque around me. I hover close to my crewmates assembled tonight on the *USS Hornet*, berthed in Alameda, California. We all breathe aloud as heaviness fills the air. I ask oceans of questions to keep any lingering spirits at bay. I've joined an evening "History Mystery Tour" on the *USS Hornet*, the CV-12 battleship, or what's left of it. Several tour attendants voice a belief in the paranormal.

"We're essentially a nineteen-story building floating on water," says Mike Gordon, one of our spook quest guides this evening. "Decks descend eight levels below the water line, and ten decks reach skyward." Mike and paranormal tour leaders plan to take us way below the water line.

The *Hornet* served as the launch for the Doolittle Raid (also called the Tokyo Raid), flinging sixteen B-25B Mitchell medium bombers, each with five crew aboard off its deck, on 18 April 1942. The raid, led by

Lieutenant Colonel James (Jimmy) Doolittle of the U.S. Air Force, retaliated against the Japanese for Pearl Harbor. While all sixteen aircraft were lost, only three crew members died. Though not a gleaming battle success, the Doolittle Raid raised U.S. military morale at all levels while cracking the Japanese spirit, say some historians.

With so much Pacific battle experience, the *USS Hornet* has a reputation as one of the most haunted warships in the U.S. Navy. Featured on several paranormal TV programs (MTV's *Fear* and the Season 3 of *JAG*), the *Hornet* boasts its own resident paranormal team, the Alameda Paranormal Researchers. Ubiquitous accounts of supernatural happenings invite many of those now present to pay the thirty-dollar fee to peer into their fear.

One middle-aged woman on tonight's tour recounts it's her third time on the ghost tour. She's accompanied by her teenage daughter this evening. As we chat, she opens the photo gallery on her iPhone and displays a shot of her middle school son with a blue luminescent orb the size of a water polo ball floating about his head—on board the *Hornet*.

"This photo was taken three years ago when we visited the ship." I glance immediately above my head. Nothing ...yet. I scan the darkening room. It's only eight o'clock. The spooks may be just waking up.

"Now hear this. Now hear this. Time to switch. Time to switch positions." I jump. The lead guide's voice over the speaker could scare anyone. Shadows grow denser in the hangar hold.

"Let's start our journey to see who's about tonight. Oh, that beam over there is where Eddie hanged himself." And who is Eddie? A member of the restoration crew. Ah. Full disclosure.

We wend our way down excruciatingly narrow metal steps—it's a battleship, so of course it has tortuous stairs. We enter the galley and mess hall.

"Pull down a chair, each of you," says Mike. "We'll be here a while."

Mike and co-paranormals Andronike and Heidi set up three flashlights (Mini Maglite 2-Cell AA Xenons) by turning the torches on, then ever so slightly twisting the caps until the light shuts off. The room is dark save for a power supply light on the side. The ghost detector guides explain that when energy moves in the room— a spirit or the ghost of a former sailor, for example— that force can switch the flashlight on or off. Others in the group set up their K-II EMF meters, a.k.a. K2 meters—devices that sense the radio frequencies of energized objects or persons (ghost energy) nearby.

Ten of us perch on the edge of hard Naugahyde chairs. We sit in close proximity, though the mess hall commands a large space. We stare at the darkness in the adjoining mess room.

"In this room, we've seen a white amorphous figure. It's white and misty," Heidi recounts.

"Yes," agrees the woman on tour for the third

time. "I have seen misty shapes in this room." I see nothing but the glow from the Maxwell House coffee maker against the right-side wall.

"Is there anyone here who would like to say hello?" Heidi enquires, projecting her voice toward the darkened room.

"If I whistle, will you whistle back?" Mike entreats the spirit.

Mike whistles again.

Expectation hangs in the air. We sit still as ice.

The word "guess" floats into sound.

"What do you want us to guess?" Mike asks, no shirker he.

Silence.

"If you hear us, why don't you turn on the light?"

The flashlight flickers, then the beam grows stronger, brighter.

Morse code taps out of the flashlight, transmitted by Heidi.

"Yikes!" Someone jumps. We all mumble a laugh, a nervous ha-ha.

"Can you duplicate the code on the flashlight for us?" Goodness, these ghostbusters do challenge the poor spirits.

"If you'd like us to leave, can you give some indication?" Heidi attempts to elicit a response from the energy force.

Footsteps sound from the unlit corridor, our way out of the mess hall. I definitely hear footsteps.

"Who's there? Who are you?" Heidi and Mike ask in unison, turning around to the opposite corridor.

After about ten minutes of sitting in the mess hall, the paranormal team commands us to move on.

We head toward the sickbay and the wounded ward, where we sit on narrow lumpy beds, stacked two high (a luxury because healthy sailor quarters sport foursome stacks of bunks). We're reminded that men who slept here had disease, broken bones, burns, contagion, and battle wounds. Pitch blackness piles up morose thoughts. Off to the side is the "Quiet Room," a chamber for dying sailors. Four bunks, straddled with bent-wire tubing, were meant for burn victims and dying sailors for a peaceful exit from this world.

"I definitely don't feel good in here tonight," says Heidi, stepping up and over the door frame. We all remain immobile, frozen.

Mike changes the subject. "The weirdest place to sleep on the *Hornet* is the Junior Officer's bunkroom forward on the ship. One bunk in that room offers the most hassle against a good night's sleep on this ship."

Mike presses on, his audience now rapt. "Initial weird experiences began with the original restoration crew because the Junior Officer's bunkroom was one of the few clean areas on the ship." Men who slept in the bunk reported being shoved and pushed out. One fellow reported being very warm as if someone slept on top of him. The restoration team stopped sleeping in that bunk. One fellow left his backpack on the bed at night. When he awoke, he found all of the contents laid out very neatly on the bed.

"We discover this spirit does not want anyone in his bed, and he's a neat freak," Mike sums up.

After six months of touching nothing on the bunk, a crew chief set his alarm clock on it so he'd have to get out of bed to turn it off in the morning. In the middle of the night, all of the sleepers heard a crash. The next morning, the crew chief overslept, then found his alarm clock scattered in a hundred pieces behind an air-conditioner across the room.

Next area to visit: The engine room, where the restoration crew member had hung himself. I feel this chamber's definite toxic vibes, particularly when we disable all possible lights.

The engine room leads up and over steel steps to the Officer's Mess. Here, I witness a Maglite flashlight roll back and forth several times on a flat counter, finally resting at the edge. In this room, one device programmed to translate energy noises into words repeats "Set. Sorry. Set. Sorry."

We march over metal barriers projecting from the ship's floor (ingress doors to prevent water from rushing into a room). Our final location for ghost detection: the flight command chamber where the squadron commander meted out orders for bombing missions.

We occupy chairs facing a curved desk and the blackboard. The stage for orders to kill and bomb. Evil actions.

"People have reported being touched physically in this room," Mike says cheerfully.

Please, not me, I think. I don't want to believe in spooks. I note that I am holding my breath.

"Hi, is anyone here?" asks Andronike.

"Who is here tonight?" Heidi queries.

We watch Mike lay his turned off Maglite on the right side of the desk. After a few seconds, the light turns on and the flashlight rolls a full three feet to the left in the curve of the desk. It halts, blinking. On leaving the room, I check the desk's surface. It's flat.

"Now hear this. Now hear this. Time to move. Time to move. Your tour of duty is over. Return to the hangar."

I inhale. We can leave.

The *Hornet*'s planes supported the U.S. landing at Okinawa and sank the Japanese battleship *Yamato.* The ship endured many a torpedo, shot down two hundred and fifty-five Japanese planes in a month, and continues to hide many scars.

I stand in the bleak hangar at ten o'clock on a dark night as the tour closed. The *USS Hornet* can certainly claim to be haunted with so many guns, so many deaths, so many unhappy times on its journey nigh.

FACT: War is not a good option to resolve conflict, yet it seems to be humans' first choice. How can we solve a situation by blowing up buildings with people and nonhuman animals inside. Military expenditures such as fuel, equipment, and supply chain operations use vast quantities of energy that pollutes the planet. The U.S. military now recognizes that climate change poses a threat to national security and the well-being of the American people.

A Constant

war ships
    ghost ships

    destruction
    obstruction

    creatures, concrete, chaos
        cloudburst downpour

    is Peaceable Kingdom
        only a painting

The Okunoin Cemetery in Koyosan hosts over 200,000 tombstones. Koyasan is the resting place of Kobo Daishi, founder of Shingon Buddhism.

Nun for a Day:
Wandering in Koyasan

Japan

At two thirty in the morning, I sprinted to the two glowing vending machines I'd spied upon our arrival earlier that day. One humming behemoth offered chilled Asahi Extra Dry; the other, canned sake for three yen—three cents U.S. I pounded the sake button after plunking in three coins. I'd just escaped from my three asynchronously snoring roommates—think slamming pile drivers interspersed with full running buzz saws *inside* your bedroom. I gulped the cool brew. Bawdy laughter reverberated at the other end of the hall. *Make that two cans of sake*, I thought as I dropped in another three yen.

Thus began my two-night stay in the Henjoson-in Temple in search of enlightenment. Raised Catholic, I'd tinkered with the idea of joining a nunnery when I was young and impressionable, and I still wondered if I could ever live a monastic life, a life so far removed from my own. I imagined a Buddhist nun's practice to resemble that of a Church novice. A serene daily practice:

chanting at sunrise, no emails, no demanding texts, no shopping, no Netflix—just quietude laced with a continuous, sonorous hum amid deep breaths of cool mountain air. But clearly, I may have not thought these images through; my journey had already required me to call upon unfamiliar rice-wine spirits on my path toward the sacred.

Chance had cast the Koyasan visit at my soon-to-be sock-covered feet. My brief excursion in Japan included a two-night stay in the Henjoson-in Monastery, the birthplace of Shingon Buddhism, nestled among the southern Japan highlands just south of Osaka. I yearned for a transcendent and transforming experience, ostensibly to build my karmic currency against petty touristic materialism and to experience a respite from my harried life. I wanted what the quintessential reformed aesthete Oscar Wilde was rumored to have said: "To have no yesterday and no tomorrow. To forget time, to forgive life, to be at peace."

I arrived in Japan after a recent visit to rural Ohio. There, I had visited with my Aunt Rose. So robust and spry at nearly ninety years, she was the last living relative of my parents' generation. On the flight over the Pacific, I'd reviewed our jovial photos taken on her well-worn sofa. My port of entry, Tokyo, was the antithesis of the slow, laconic pace of eastern Ohio where I grew up. However, the gentle breezes surrounding Koyasan and its one quiet main street served as a strong reminder of home.

My pilgrimage to the Kii Mountains started with frantic subway hopping during Tokyo's rush hour. We next streamed onto the high-speed bullet train, the Tōhoku Shinkansen, speeding to Kyoto at two hundred miles per hour. Snatching the next express train to Hashimoto with four minutes to spare, we had a luxurious nine minutes to snag a third train for the final leg of the journey, the Koyasan cable car up to Mount Koya.

At the top of the incline, I strode out of the tram station into a white-furled mist that swirled around my shivering body. It was as if I'd just stepped into the gauzed cut of a film by Kurosawa. Muted winds whispered past my ears; fog fingers held my face. The air smelled phosphorescent. I inhaled the fresh scent of ancient cedar. The wind conversed with a garbled insouciance. I waited for the white-faced, toothless ghosts from *Ran*, Kurosawa's rendering of *King Lear*, to emerge at any moment as I searched for the front gate of Henjoson-in Temple, one of more than a hundred temples that lace the mountain.

On Mount Koya, we declined a taxi, deciding to idle toward the town as dusk settled. Signage was nearly nonexistent along the road, and the building numbers that lit door frames in kanji were indecipherable to me. Lugging minimalist luggage—what could a Buddhist nun possibly need for a two-day stay?—I wandered through the town past the temple at least three times before several members of our group congregated at the main gate.

The massive wooden door of Henjoson-in welcomed us, and a raked sand lawn hailed our entry. A genial monk greeted us in English, escorting our entourage into the monastery after first requesting that we remove shoes on the outer porch for the night. The rooms were dressed in traditional Japanese décor; tea sat hot and ready on the low table. Futons floated about the floor, each covered with an orange down comforter. The bathroom proffered a fine rectangular cedar tub, its deep earthy scent inviting me to turn on the tap. Donning a robe and the two-toed white socks and *zōri* sandals every respectable monk and nun must wear, my feet flapped to the central dining room.

Abruptly, a handsome temple monk appeared out of nowhere. Hand signals and anxious tones replaced civilized dialog. Another monk arrived and translated: I had committed *machigai*, the faux pas of wearing the kimono-that-must-remain-in-the-room. It was never to be worn to dinner. I scuttled back to the room to change. No operating instructions had accompanied the robes.

Back in our private dining hall properly attired, sitting flat on the floor, I opened the box placed in front of me. An acetic scent stung my nasal passages. Lively oranges and bright greens suspended my appetite. Every meal served in Koyasan Buddhist monasteries is vegetarian—*shojin ryori*. Strong aromatic vegetables such as garlic or onion are anathema. Each supplicant received this deep-red partitioned box with assorted non-meat items gaily presented. I did recognize the miso sloshing in the requisite lacquer bowl as well as the reassuring white rice. Presently, I ate everything as any grateful nun would, even the briny orange rubbery substance that none of my fellow diners would touch. Rather chewy and salty, infused with vinegar, I swallowed hard, noting to avoid this dish if it was ever served again.

After dinner, all guests headed off to rest on those glorious futons. A communal bath was offered: one for men, one for women. I gave in to a languid impulse and rode the disability chair up the stairway. I disembarked, but the chair stuck at the top of the landing, unable to descend. I motioned the problem to the tall young monk nearby. He promptly came over and kicked the recalcitrant device, and it wobbled back down its track. After surveying the crowded women's bath, I descended the stairs on my own two feet and had a soak in the private cedar tub.

Fully relaxed after the hot bath, I nestled between the floor futon and the bright ginger kakefuton. Darkness poured through the floor-to-ceiling windows. My suitemates settled themselves, eventually, into deep loud snoring.

Back to the vending machines and my two a.m. meditation. I stared at the neon glow for twenty minutes. The monastery had quieted. Retracing my steps to my room, I listened outside the rattan panel. The inhabitants of this room had finally quieted too. Gazing into the darkness outside the window, a small rabbit appeared and skipped the grounds, later to enter my dreams appealing for peace and contentment.

Kappoonnngg! Raucous vibrations sped from my ears through my chest and into the pit of my stomach. At five thirty that morning, the temple gong boomed and we were spirited to the altar room and chanting hall. Three monks knelt with their backs to the visitors and began an intonation. They intensified their deep throaty song, their sutras, soaring into a solid rocking rhythm. After an hour of sitting very still and reeling in my mind from its flight to the polished wooden rafters, the main monk—he who wore the most colorful garb— turned and addressed the attendees. Bald and rotund, he smiled wider and wider. I only understood a few words of Japanese: *arigato* translates to "thank you" and *Koyasan* meant, well, Koyasan. But it was abundantly apparent that he welcomed all of us devotees, supplicants, and chanters no matter why we sat with him and his two accompanists.

Through hand motions, deep kowtows, and wide smiles, we were instructed to follow a path down wooden steps into the monastery basement. Stepping on outlined stones, I followed the movements of every other tourist. Stop, bow at a rectangular glass jar, side-wise step. Repeat. We honored each clear glass box along the shelved wall. Hundreds of these urns lined the walls. They were filled to the brim with brown-gray powder and stones. I intuited and later confirmed that these oblong vessels held the ashes of departed monks.

Unnamed yet honored by countless visiting worshipers over hundreds of years.

Following this walk among the dead, many of us donated yen to the monastery to be permitted to copy Buddhist sutras by hand. Right to left, as instructed by the monks. I had read that *shakyo*, the meditative practice of handwriting sutras over and over, appears to counter dementia. With this in mind, I dutifully sat as a nun in training at the low table, filling in outlined kanji with a brush. Right to left, right to left. I had to fight the urge to start a new page, judging my efforts not perfect enough for the Buddha. My colleagues finished quickly, and the young Japanese couple zipped through their page. For some confounding reason, this focused task slowed my usual quick response; after a time, I found myself alone at the table and in the room, encircled in silence. Sitting among the ashes of the monks, I pondered: *why here, why now?* Why had my hand slackened in this monastic space?

The consciousness of death remains an integral part of life in Japan. Even death's approach has produced a centuries-old tradition of death poems— jisei. A few years before this Japan visit, my son had honored my love of poetry by gifting me with a collection entitled *Japanese Death Poems*, written by Zen monks and haiku poets. While I had wondered about his choice of anthologies (for Christmas—really?), upon exploring the volume, the tradition of writing a farewell poem to life seemed cathartic and entirely natural. It is simply part of the continuum of dying that exists in Japan. Some Zen Buddhists believe a dead person does not enter a place of no return immediately upon dying, imagining their relative's spirit to hover on the border of eternity for decades, even centuries. This allows them to visit the gravesite and chat with the deceased, relating family happenings, emotional revelations, or even daily events.

As the ghosts of monks past surrounded me, my phone, which I'd been spiritually unable to part with that day, buzzed with a text from my cousin Jim. My dear Aunt Rose had been hospitalized and was not doing well. In the past week, she'd suffered health setbacks and discovered she had cancer. The vibrant woman who I'd sat next to on the sofa just weeks earlier suddenly moved on a different path.

I set down the pen-brush and left my painted-in sutras on the table. Perfection at a single task such as this seemed an elusive ambition that truly did not matter in the infinite universe we inhabit. I climbed the planked stairs in silence.

Each day at Koyasan, the monks present morning offerings at six-thirty a.m. for Kūkai (also known as Kōbō Daishi or "The Great Teacher of the Vast Karma"). Kūkai introduced Shingon Buddhism to Japan more than fourteen centuries ago. He spoke of three secret mysteries to his devotees: the secrets of the body, of speech, and of mind. Kūkai taught that the human body symbolizes the larger universe, that reciting voiced mantras expresses truths, and that looking inward leads to a place of non-activity and peace.

Kūkai's followers believe his spirit continues to enjoy the vegetarian fare placed in a large shrouded chest and ferried up to his mausoleum by monks wearing masks to conceal their faces. Visitors are welcomed to the daybreak ceremony.

The next morning, after the one-hour of chanting and an unrecognizable breakfast, I walked toward Okunoin Cemetery, where Kūkai's mausoleum rests at the far end. To reach the wooden temple over his grave, I passed two hundred thousand grave markers of all materials—concrete, wood, fabric, and metal—gathered at random amid soaring cedars. Stopping frequently to admire cloth decorations on statues or read the Mitsubishi company's dedications, I felt at home among these memorials to the dead.

As I approached Kūkai's resting place, another text jangled my cell phone. What would this new message impart to me here, halfway across the planet? Again, from cousin Jim: his mother, my Aunt Rose, had just died. As my footsteps halted at the base of the mausoleum, I instantly relived my last visit with her. She had joked about politics, her health problems, the beauty of her garden. "She has no more pain. We are grateful," Jim signed off. Basho, Japan's esteemed haiku poet, wrote his death poem four days before he died:

On a journey, ill;
my dream goes wandering
over withered fields.

I felt blessed to be in Koyasan in the company of my dear aunt's global counterparts. As tears ran down my face, I wandered slowly, meditating on the deep spiritual moment of living the life of a Buddhist nun if only for one day. I vowed when I returned to Ohio, I would visit Aunt Rose's grave and carry to her the offerings of poppyseed bread and pierogi, the Polish comfort foods of our clan. I would speak to her reverently, joyfully. She would relish an update on my travels and the profound and limitless nature of the world.

FACT: A short stay in a Japanese monastery introduced me to ghosts who taught me acceptance of fellow humans and nonhuman animals. And letting go of expectations. I walked through the cemetery of two hundred thousand headstones and monuments expecting to find Aunt Rose's column.

Immortality

headstones in
   the Kii mountains
   wave to be counted

storms surrounded by
   brewing death
   seas rising

I pray
   for Aunt Rose
      walking the hills

Fly away! Parahawking near Pokhara, Nepal, and feeding Kevin, an Egyptian vulture. Once in the air, initial fears were replaced by the wonder of flying.

Parahawking:
Seeing the World Anew

Nepal

When I hit sixty, my eldest daughter said, "Sixty is the new forty." These words spawned in me a wanderlust the likes of which I couldn't believe, and weeks after my birthday I challenged myself to go alone to Antarctica. After cavorting with flocks of frenzied penguins and climbing out of a dormant volcano, I returned to Ushuaia in Tierra del Fuego and an email bearing the news that my ninety-one-year-old father was fading fast. I rushed from Argentina to Ohio to hold his hand for the last five days of his life. I never did tell him, a great watcher of birds, about my adventure with the penguins he would have so loved.

After witnessing my father's death, I resolved to live more fully in each moment. My most vivid moments come when I'm somewhere new, moving through uncharted waters or land or air. Not only did I commit to hitting the road more frequently each year, but I pledged to my father's memory to let go of fears that, at sixty, still held me back.

I have a particular fear of heights. Even Ferris wheels stop me cold. My breath freezes whenever the bucket pauses at the top. I have peered warily at the London Eye, never gathering the gumption to purchase a ticket; similarly, I have always adamantly refused to look down from the Empire State Building, and when flying, I automatically select an aisle seat.

However, having watched my father face death with grace and courage, I vowed to face life without the reticence and trepidation that had tugged at me for a lifetime. It was in this spirit of abandon that I pulled a running jump (with some help from a launch crew) off nearly mile high Sarangkot Mountain in Pokhara, Nepal to parahawk with a bird named Kevin.

Before I went to Nepal, the concept of parahawking had never entered my consciousness. British falconer Scott Mason and his crew created this hybrid of falconry and paragliding in 2001, melding adventure with conservation. The Parahawking Project educates participants on hawk and vulture flight behavior and how these birds survive in the wild. Through para-hawking tandem rides, the organization raises funds to restore the nearly decimated vulture population in Nepal.

Vultures have an enduring image problem. People often envision them circling above a nearly dead animal, ready to dive in once it heaves its last breath. Besides the resulting general distaste for these creatures, a crisis occurred in the late 1990s when Nepalese, Indian, and Pakistani farmers, as a compassionate gesture, treated their farm animals with the anti-inflammatory diclofenac to reduce their pain as they aged. These creatures eventually died in the open and, as the many varieties of Asian vultures rid the streets of the carrion, the diclofenac-laced flesh poisoned the birds, and their numbers decreased precipitously.

Parahawking consists of tandem paragliding while feeding water buffalo meat to a large raptor. I hung suspended in a bag seat while Scott, a seasoned British paraglider and expert falconer, sat behind me and operated the guidelines and controls. On my maiden flight, I paired with Kevin, a trained white-feathered Egyptian vulture whose black-tipped white wings were a stunning sight to behold, spanning five-and-a-half feet.

Kevin was a rescue bird. The Egyptian vulture, which inhabits southern Europe, northern Africa, and western and southern Asia, is one of ten species nearing extinction. On Phewa Lake, Scott's base and home to his young family, Kevin demonstrated his species' expertise in the use of tools by dropping rocks onto an egg to crack the shell. His thin beak and long neck allowed him to claim carrion that larger birds could not.

Choosing to fly off a cliff was not my usual modus operandi. I required a slight coaxing. Christina, the organizer of my Nepal expedition, encouraged me. "They haven't lost anyone yet," she said. *But there's always the first time*, I thought.

However, my sixty-year-old new resolve allowed another rather surprising thought: *If I must die someday, soaring through the unseen wind currents above the white-capped Annapurnas will be as lovely a place as any.*

In the days leading up to my flight, I continued exploring the sites around Pokhara, panting my way up to the Shanti Stupa, or Peace Pagoda, the Buddhist shrine on an island in Phewa Lake adjoining Pokhara. The stunning Annapurnas kept me in the present.

My only instructions for parahawking were: Leap off the cliff and keep running in case the chute doesn't open. *Right.* My mind pressed my legs to move through the powerful gusts of wind. However, matter over mind won, and I slammed back into my harness seat. A crewmember had to help our tandem launch by essentially tossing the pilot and me over the cliff. Then we were off, circling the Sarangkot with two dozen other paragliders.

In flight, we soared with the enormous birds, following their movements to catch updrafts and keep our chute apparatus aloft. The eyesight of birds betters that of humans by ten to fifteen times. Their keen eyes identified the swirls of dust defining drafts and currents that were invisible to me on this bright, blue-sky day.

While we were suspended in the air, time stopped. Scott swooped up and whistled for Kevin. The graceful great vulture made his approach to my outstretched, leather-gloved hand that held his treat. He gently retrieved the fresh-cut water buffalo chunk that would fuel his long journeys through the air. We repeated this scene many times. I filled my lungs fully throughout each of the thirty minutes aloft.

One abrupt updraft did surprise me. I had to close my eyes and trust my pilot during a quick right jolt and ascent. We climbed several hundred feet fast, then turned, and the entire snow-capped Annapurna range spread out before us, a heavenly vision.

Under a sky resplendent with multi-colored chutes, I found I had no time to even consider my fear. Our half-hour flight ended so gently. Much like Kevin, we glided to a small patch of grass bordering Phewa Lake, smack dab across the road from the impressive Maya Devi Temple. Enlightenment indeed.

I find myself agreeing more and more with my sometime travel companion, an Australian septuagenarian whose motto is: "Comfort travel doesn't interest me." If anything, I now seek *discomfort* travel or travel that offers me opportunities to confront my fears, push my boundaries, expand my worldview, and build trust and connections with my fellow creatures on this earth.

I hear some people speak of bucket lists and thousands of places to see before they leave this earth, as if travel exists as a checklist to complete. I find that each second spent traveling breathes life into the following moment of time and place. I now see the distinct shape of each leaf on the trees lining my street and inhale the scent of cantaloupe in my local market with gratitude. I meditate while watching the birds gliding above my San Francisco home. Travel deepens one's senses and sense of self. It lengthens and stretches out the time we have to challenge ourselves to begin anew, each day to rise above this earth.

FACT: A blinding snowstorm canceled my flight out of Katmandu. In a hotel, I met a premier Chinese mountain climber and his touring team. He'd ascended the highest peaks on all seven continents. His group spokesperson said they had attended a Himalaya conference of representatives from Nepal, India, China, and Pakistan. Scientists found that the snowpack had become wetter during the past several seasons, a possible reason for so many recent climbing deaths and avalanches.

Still Snow

warming snow
melts resolve
 to scale
  any peak
warmed by
  a heating planet
     yet
many still
reach out to
  nirvana
   seven peaks

Storytelling at Café Clock—in Arabic, then in English.
Listening to each other and laughing together builds
community and joy.

An Evening at Café Clock

Morocco

"Ya omena mule. Habed to non sanada." Staccato sounds in a language I did not know hit my ears in Café Clock, a boisterous bistro and gathering place in the Fes medina. Moroccans in attendance guffawed and chortled. I had no idea what the storyteller—black tam rakishly askew on his head, swaying in the center of the room—spouted to his visibly adoring audience. I'm enthralled as well. I'm hooked as I sit in a *hulka*, a Moroccan storytelling circle. We're huddled in the packed street-level room of Café Clock, a popular destination restaurant in Fes, a World Heritage Site. The aroma of Arabic spices—the *ras al hanout*, caramelized onions, and lamb tagine cooked with summer vegetables—wafted through the air. Camel burgers with *taza* ketchup and fries float by on waiters' trays. The mint bouquet of sugared tea floated upward, reaching the colored glass ceiling.

I relished just finding the place. The excitement inside was worth the effort to get there. I'd have never located the hopping cantina again if left to my internal GPS. The official address: 7 Derb el Magana, Fes, Morocco. Right. Street signage is rare in the Fes medina. Hand-scrawled makeshift placards or faded nailed wooden notices are often the only directions for visitors. Most are tacked to an upper wall on a winding alley.

We entered the medina of the Fez labyrinth through the Blue Gate—Grande Porte Bab Bou Jeloud. That's where my brain's usually excellent space tracker ended and my GPS fritzed. Friends directed, "Café Clock is off the Tala Khabira, the big main road." I would not use the word "road." We wended our way over a slippery path of sorts. After a few twists and turns and the final move through an extremely narrow passageway—*voila*! There sprung the entrance door to Café Clock.

Travel guides claim the Café Clock is near the Madrasa Bou Inania, a school founded in 1822 and full of ecstatic mosaics, cedar geometric cupolas, and carved tiles of Qur'an couplets. Café Clock was also supposed to be quite close to the remains of Fes's once-functional medieval water clock, now reposed in ruin. What guidebooks don't divulge is that one must turn left at the fishmonger's stall (ah, now I see the why of the slippery path) and crouch through a dark, single-person-wide low alley to arrive at the eatery and gathering place.

"The Clock," as some call it, churns with a cauldron of visitors, expatriates, and local Moroccans. The restaurant occupies several levels, as do many buildings in the Fes medina. Assorted terraces command city views. The climb to the upper floors is so steep that a waiter would require mountain-climbing experience on their resume.

Café Clock bounded from the heart of the inexorably smiling Mike Richardson, hailing from Yorkshire, England. Mike fell in love with Morocco and its people years earlier and became especially fond of Fes and the sacred city of Moulay Idriss. In London, he'd served as maître d' at The Ivy and The Wolseley eateries. The beautiful foods and ingredients he witnessed in the medina sealed his move to the North African country. His launch of Café Clock provided a venue for the resurgence of storytelling by a seasoned master and a rebirth of this art form through the training of young apprentices.

Storyteller Mohammed Mokhlis, handsome in his close-fitting beret, mesmerized the Café Clock crowd as he sputtered an Arabic anecdote through his salt-and-pepper beard. His good looks, twinkling eyes, and slight smile belied his seventy years. He regaled the tourist assembly. His body movements gyrated through his gravel voice. Not understanding a word of what he said did not diminish the pleasure of the experience. I found myself smiling, rapt with fascination about whatever tale he was telling. The Moroccan and Arabic speakers in the room laughed and giggled as Mokhlis paused, winking often to the side tables. Eventually, I would hear the story. When this aged Moroccan storyteller completed his performance, a young millennial apprentice who majored in English at the university stood up and retold the story in my native language, all the while mirroring their mentor's body movements, pauses, laughs, and wise-look finale.

According to Zakia Elyoubi, an apprentice to Mokhlis for nearly five years, the master raconteur's yarn told of a man whose wife had just died. Mokhlis punctuated each statement with a long stop (I so wish you'd have been in the room). The couple had been married for forty years. The wife's family and friends carried her body to the graveyard as is proper. The pallbearers hoisted the wife's coffin on their shoulders, solemnly following the path to the cemetery. The husband trailed, and then he began to laugh and laugh, loudly, during the funeral procession. Not the usual decorum for a Moroccan funeral. The story ended as Mokhlis said what sounded like *"Deems suden molas."* Then he added (again what sounded like), *"Nom shad, com ta nateedaed."* The Moroccan audience murmured and then exploded in laughter.

I rocked in rhythm to Mokhlis's words and the onlookers' hilarity. I found myself swaying back and forth and tittering as well. Zakia, sitting nearby, burst into rapturous laughter for several minutes before she could speak again.

Zakia stood and translated the tale. "People shouted, 'What's wrong with him?! Why is he laughing at his wife's funeral procession? His wife just died, and he's laughing! Why are you laughing? Your wife just died! Are you crazy?!'"

The old husband then answered, "I was married to her for forty years—forty years! And today is the first time I know where she is going!" Zakia laughed and laughed; the Moroccan audience guffawed. A huge smile crept across my face.

The beehive that is Fes convinced me that all inhabitants are sisters and brothers in the eyes of the ancients who proscribed laughter as the first emotion felt among creatures inhabiting the planet. Stories act to loosen the space between us. It's as if unknotting a string of yarn not by yanking or jerking but by a loose fondling, a soft pull of mindaro green, golden amber, and mauve among the dancing lights. Not understanding the words presented no problem in understanding the story's intent. It didn't stop me or other non-Arabic speakers from joining in the merriment. Laughing together with all in the room, we had gelled into a community. Laughing aloud felt so good at Café Clock.

FACT: Morocco's deforestation for agriculture and animal grazing invites negative climate consequences, increases water pollution, and decreases wildlife species. Water scarcity, food insecurity, desertification, shoreline erosion, and climate migration create more environmental stress. Yet young storytellers practice in the footsteps of their masters, inviting laughter and community to resolve the planet's problems.

Footsteps

a new generation
  of storytellers
retell the plague
  of species
   extinction
  scarcity

  the monk seal
  calls to the gazelle
      don't betray your heart

The ancient Greeks revered the octopus. This jar, on display in the National Archaeological Museum of Athens dates back to the fifteenth century BCE.

Know Thyself:
The Octopus and Me

Greece

I used to eat octopus. In fact, I used to *love* eating octopus—grilled or ceviche—until I learned that these soft-bodied mollusks get amorous on ecstasy. Yes, ecstasy: the drug. Scientists at Johns Hopkins University recently dosed a consortium (the collective name for a group of octopuses) of the eight-armed creatures with the drug we call methylenedioxymethamphetamine, MDMA, Molly, X, or candy. Researchers discovered that when given a high dose of the drug, the treated invertebrates would huddle alone in a corner of their tank. But when dosed with a small quantity—the equivalent amount to what a human would ingest—those same octopuses transformed into empathetic, cuddly social beings.

When placed in an aquarium together, octopuses usually demonstrate aggressive behavior to tank mates. They color-shift and turn dark hues, cobalt-blue or ink-black. The attacker stands tall on several tentacles, often shooting a solitary appendage toward its adversary, lashing out much the way they're depicted in horror films. But ecstasy-treated octopuses sidle up to their fellow cephalopods, slowly exploring the environment, caressing toys, and using several arms. These responses strikingly resemble human behavioral changes when on the drug. In people, ecstasy decreases anxiety and inhibitions, generates empathy and compassion, and enriches the physical senses. In octopuses, the investigators witnessed a long-considered aggressive monster of the deep become an affectionate creature full of touchy-feely strokes for rivals.

After reading the study, I couldn't help but seek out documentary evidence of these incredible findings. My inner scientist simply had to know what octopus "love behaviors" looked like.

Little did I know that my quick online video search would deter me from ever again eating an octopus. A plethora of films abound with octopus caresses. But I found so much more: an octopus unscrewing a jar, mimicking a flounder, and, most precious of all, pretending to be a piece of coral.

One video showed a rather large golden-brown octopus sliding in the surf along with a family who had rescued this creature the day before. The animal had come back to the same beach and spent an hour with them as they strolled across the sand. Another recording revealed a small octopus being released into the ocean after having been stranded at low tide, then returning to thank the human who released it. The octopod placed its tentacle gently atop the foot of its savior, stayed still for a minute as if in silent prayer, then pushed out to the sea. Heart-rending.

This simple act of connection and cross-species empathy nailed shut the coffin of my octopus-eating days. My throat tightened; my stomach clenched. No more. I could never be at ease with eating octopus again.

My culinary sea change has evolved, as with any evolutionary timetable, over decades. I journey all over the world and enjoy local delicacies as part of my travel writing vocation. How could I renounce octopus, whether served in Greece, Japan, or the Caribbean— where octopus is considered a local delicacy? A friend recently told me about being served a "baby octopus" on her plate while visiting Japan. "So delicious," she sighed. I wept at this story.

The foundations of my evolutionary change occurred in the fall of 1994 when my then-ten-year-old daughter informed me matter-of-factly that she was a vegetarian. "Why?" I asked. "I don't want to eat anything that has a face." While I was a bit miffed that I'd have to cook a separate menu for her, my daughter's announcement set my brain whirring. Should I, too, be feeling bad for eating be-faced creatures? Was my daughter morally superior to me? Would I have to learn how to cook tofu? How would I supply her with protein?

Mainstream culinary culture has taken a quarter-century to catch up with my daughter. In 2000, Harvard Law School acceded to student demand and established an animal law course. Many law schools across the

United States followed suit. In 2002, Germany amended its constitution to raise the protection of nonhuman animals to a fundamental level.

Over the past several years, I've become profoundly grateful that humans, myself included, have become enlightened about the consciousness and feelings of all creatures. On July 7, 2012, the Cambridge Declaration on Consciousness proclaimed a universal proclamation on animal sentience. This group of cognitive and computational neuroscientists had assembled to proclaim that nonhuman animals, including the great apes, dolphins, elephants, birds, and octopuses, possess pathways throughout their brains that show emotional feelings. Just because an animal doesn't have a neocortex like a human doesn't mean they can't feel. Octopuses have "neurological substrates" shared by *Homo sapiens* that generate consciousness even though the two species diverged on the tree of life about six hundred million years ago. And look very different to the outside world.

While I fully supported these strides in animal welfare and seriously cut down on my meat consumption, I wasn't ready to give up on all meats. More significantly, I knew there were still some gastronomies I had yet to encounter.

On my first Greek voyage to the southern Peloponnesus in 2007, I discovered the gastronomic delights of the octopus. Each day at sunrise, I sat in tranquil meditation, gazing over the morning catch of octopuses drying out on the glass lampposts. Their voluptuous forms adorned every streetlamp up and down the embarcadero. A saltfish smell wafted up into the street cafes from the peaceful blue-green waves lapping over the seawall.

Nearing noon every day, the charcoal fires flickered in front of the tavernas lining the *paraliakó diádromo*. Smoke swirled upward from the burning coals, enticing the passersby. I was no exception. Previously, I'd despised octopus dishes with a vengeance because of the rubbery consistency that's ubiquitous in the United States. But in Greece, I experienced an epicurean heaven of soft-textured, melt-in-the-mouth, succulent, juicy rings. Each was cooked to a precise point of perfection.

In Neapoli, Hellenic cooks expertly chopped the mollusks into exacting sections, roasting these morsels with a drizzle of olive oil and a dash of salt. I ate at the same taverna each day with friends, placing the same order from the same menu: ouzo and charcoal-broiled octopus.

At the time, I unwittingly endorsed Aristotle's twenty-four-century-old opinion: "The octopus is a stupid creature...for it will approach a man's hand if it be lowered in the water." Thankfully, human knowledge has evolved since the time of Aristotle. We now know empirically that the octopus is not the least bit stupid. With three hearts and nine brains, studies of octopus's acumen continue to reveal new insights into this species. And as my YouTube deep-dive confirmed, when an octopus explores an extended hand, it's showing curiosity and courage. The octopus does not shrink from learning what the hand represents.

Over the past several years, I've become profoundly grateful that humans, myself included, are becoming increasingly enlightened about the consciousness and feelings of all creatures. In addition to the Cambridge Declaration on Consciousness on animal sentience, we've learned that while the octopus genome isn't quite as large as a human's, it contains a greater number of protein-coding genes—about 33,000, compared to fewer than 25,000 of these genes in *Homo sapiens*. This abundance of protein-coding genes allows octopuses to respond quickly to their environment with an aptitude that humans don't possess. As Stephen Hawking has said about humans, "We are just an advanced breed of monkeys on a minor planet of a very average star. But we can understand the Universe. That makes us something very special." Special enough to treat our fellow creatures with consideration and compassion. The more I learned about octopuses, the more I vowed to never eat them again.

In *Animal Rights: What Everyone Needs to Know*, Paul Waldau chronicles the timeline for human-animal interactions spanning 35,000 years. From the 20,000-year-old cave drawings at Lascaux, France, to the Treaties of Amsterdam and Rome in the late 1990s that established laws defining nonhuman animals as "sentient beings," animal rights have gained credence.

During my latest visit to Greece, in 2019, I carried within me a new understanding of this sea creature's consciousness. I prayed that these beings didn't have an existential memory of me devouring dozens of their kin on the Neapoli shores and hoped they understood how boldly I now celebrated their intelligence.

On this recent trip, the day before a hosted luncheon at the renowned Imerovigli Restaurant in Piraeus—renowned for its octopus and squid—I made a pilgrimage to the Temple of Apollo at Delphi. Hoping to breathe in the methane and carbon dioxide vapors that scientists now think allowed female oracles to predict and proscribe the future for ancient Greeks, I meditated on the weighty Greek aphorism, "Know thyself." Inscribed on the pronaos of Apollo's Temple, this maxim has been ascribed to playwright Aeschylus in *Prometheus Bound*, to Socrates as he wrote his history *Memorabilia*, and to Plato, who used his characterization of Socrates for this motivational axiom. Whether it was the ninety-five-degree temperatures in the direct sun of high noon that day at Delphi or the methane miasma seeping up around me, I reaffirmed my resolve. I had to honor my new understanding of and compassion for the octopus.

On the next day of my enlightenment, I decided not to dine on the creatures. At the luncheon at the

Imerovigli, the memories of the potent flavors and soft texture from thirteen years prior didn't even tempt me to taste the fragrant grilled slices. Despite my slight embarrassment at refusing the host's offerings, I stood strong. As we sat in the open air above Piraeus harbor, yachts and sailboats bobbing in the noon sun and sparkling off the bluest water, I was at peace with my decision.

As a garrulous member of our party repeated an outlandish tale about a breakfast smoothie for the third time, all eyes and ears were focused on his lighthearted anecdote. At the other end of the table, I meditated on the serving plate in sadness. The magnificent beings I held in my hands were already dead, and by this logic, there might be no harm in my partaking of the char-broiled meat. But the immobile cuttlefish still looked like cuttlefish, and the squid tentacles splayed about on the plate still seemed to move. Both were cephalopods with neurological substrates of emotions and feelings shared with the octopus. I passed on the dish serving as the creature's bier.

Amid the din of lunchtime laughter and conversation, no one noticed that at one point I held the separate platter of grilled octopus in my hands for several moments. Then a whisper touched an ear.

Know thyself.

As if the Delphic oracle stood nearby.

Know thyself. And know all other creatures.

Socrates's ghost gusted past my other ear. I was momentarily taken aback.

Their spirits do reside in Greece, I reasoned. The octopus's sarcophagus weighed heavy in my hands.

In his *Philosophies,* Socrates always emphasized actions over words, and all at once I was seized by a fervent notion. I could run to the high-walled street's edge and upend the plate into the harbor—a burial at sea for these creatures lying prone in my hands.

Instead, I followed my next impulse: I quietly set the oval platter on the edge of the table and gently covered it with a white cloth napkin. The pall had been placed. I entreated past and future Greek gods for the octopuses' peaceful passage into Poseidon's realm. I thoroughly enjoyed my delightful Greek salad.

FACT: One of the pleasures of travel is experiencing new foods and dining traditions. Many international chefs now focus on food sustainability in their novel offerings across the planet. Scientists worldwide have stepped up to create renewable supercrops. They predict we all may be vegetarians in the future, as animal farming poses severe costs to the environment and overfishing the seas creates food scarcity. A plant-based diet produces significantly less carbon emissions, they advise.

Sharing

sharing the planet
all may stop
    to cogitate

searching for
mystic notions
    to vegetate

Spirit Mountain allowed "forest bathing" among open and quiet paths, to enjoy the cleansing power of trees and cool air.

Spirit Mountain

Japan

Solvitur ambulando. It is solved by walking.

—Diogenes the Cynic (412-323 BCE)

A distinct memory entered my mind on a recent walk past the San Francisco Presidio sculpture *Spire* by artist Andy Goldsworthy. In the panorama of my travels, I remember my journey up Japan's Mount Tsukuba and my wanderings through its forests. This memory shook the usual tranquility of my morning meditation walk.

Why this memory at this time?

Russian poet Osip Mandelstam thought that memories find us when we are ready to welcome them, or when we need them. I've come to believe this too. There on Mount Tsukuba, I met a Buddha. His smile revisits me often.

At a time when I could not travel, a memory resurfaces in my mind. It's a memory of a particular walk along Mount Tsukuba's forest paths outside of Kyoto that I took decades ago. As a science journalist, I'd been assigned to cover a 1996 science meeting at the Kyoto International Conference Center, a curious, striking hexagonal structure located in Takaragaike north of the city.

After listening to and recording four days of non-stop research presentations, I desperately needed to do some walking. I allowed myself a day of sightseeing before I had to scurry back to my three small children, the daily grind of parenthood, and work in San Francisco. My head craved air and some adventure in the countryside. I required strength and fortitude to reenter the hectic chaos of a household with three small ones who daily challenged my inner peace (my eldest had actually called me at my Kyoto hotel to ask "Mom, where is my black ballet leotard?").

A short train ride brought me to the foot of Mount Tsukuba. Teetering on the edge of the cable car platform in line with Japanese tourists, my memory becomes somewhat surreal and hazy. In those days, I didn't take plentiful, profuse, numerous, and copious notes when I traveled, a practice I've developed over the ensuing years.

The cable car up the mountain was painted bright yellow, akin to the Beatles' *Yellow Submarine*—cozy and sturdy-looking enough, but totally vulnerable to the elements. I stood in a quiet queue waiting to board. I'm terrified of heights. Rumbling through my mind are visions of crashing on the rocks below, tumbling through outstretched pine branches as the car tumbles down the mountain, my small body banging against the windows.

The car ascended the nearly vertical incline on a track. As I stepped off the tram onto a landing, quaint, sparse tourist shops lined the turnaround, with the shopkeepers hawking chips, tchotchkes, Hello Kitty knickknacks. The air smelled of pine and cedar; a high-pitched breeze hummed past my ears.

As if pulled by the spirit of the mountain, I headed uphill on foot toward the trees. I carried no camera. No notebook. No map. I wore a small daypack that carried only water and my passport. A few yen rested in my pocket.

At this juncture in my life, I had never heard of the Japanese penchant for *shinrin-yoku*, or forest bathing. Forest bathe I did. For nearly the entire day, starting in midmorning and straight through the evening. The live oak, Japanese cedar, mountain cherry, and red pines reached for the sky with finger-like branches. Pinene, that fragrant chemical that bestows the trees' distinctive scent, floated upward as I stepped on the soft-needled forest floor. Turpentine—was that the essence of the needle carpet I smelled?

I wandered imprecise, muffled trails, cleared of bramble and bushes but untrampled as if someone had gently swept them with a natural brush earlier that morning. Purple hydrangeas and bright red rhododendrons intermingled with the small green plants on the edges of the trails. The forest opened into spontaneous paths. I wandered down one then circled back to another, lost in time. Immersed in the Mifune and Kurosawa films over many decades, I imagined myself a samurai on a life quest.

Diogenes whispered to keep walking. It was a moving meditation to resolve daily problems, issues that seem to follow me wherever I traveled, that full catastrophe of daily living. Usually, I worried for my safety during such solitary times, but this day I trusted the universe, the forest.

I walked as an immigrant pilgrim, carrying the clothes on my back. Focused on breathing in, breathing out, I was overtaken by the mountain spirit's presence guiding my steps. Eventually, as if led by this spirit, I came upon a Buddhist temple. The building boasted bright oranges, blues, greens, and reds on dark wood columns and walls. Surprised by the temple's riots of color in the midst of the natural forest's many shades of brown and green, I stepped onto the wooden stairs and walked in. I strode into the temple and immediately came face to face with a gentle, smiling floor-to-ceiling Buddha. I estimated it to be about eighteen feet tall. I smiled back, craning my neck toward the ceiling.

Meandering through the building, no one seemed to be around. No shoes sat neatly at the bottom step. No incense or candles burned. I had the temple to myself. After years of mindfulness meditation and training, I now know I should have at least removed my shoes. Faux pas indeed.

I returned to the sculpture and stood before it, hiking boots still tied tight. Sunlight angled through the tree canopy and lit up dark corners of the temple. Weightless beams filtered in, slashing along the wall and passing over the Buddha. In the middle of a forest, I stood suspended in time and place. No monks or nuns showed up. Just me. The Buddha continued to smile. His elegant hands rested on his knees as he sat straight-backed, his soft gaze keeping me suspended in place. I forgot all my personal responsibilities. I felt as if I was in my own home or that of my parents. The scent of balsa wafted in through the airy rafters.

I continue to hike the hills near my home. I often visit *Spire* on my morning walks. It's a powerful symbol of the rejuvenation of the beloved Presidio Forest, first planted by the Army in the 1880s. The aging Monterey cypresses are approaching the end of their lives and are being replaced with healthy saplings. In 2008, Goldsworthy selected thirty-seven Monterey trunks from cypress trees felled at the site and fastened them together. Around its fifteen-foot-wide base, the forestry service planted young cypresses that will eventually grow to conceal the sculpture. This process emulates an old forest enveloping and welcoming new growth.

In June 2020, *Spire* suffered fire damage, most likely at the hand of an arsonist.

"Like many things happening at this time, the burning of *Spire* doesn't make any sense," said Goldsworthy. "What I do know is that art doesn't give up. *Spire* is still standing and is still very beautiful. It is now more rooted in the place than ever before. It will always stand there—even when it has been removed."

Much like the Buddha I met on Mount Tsukuba, *Spire*'s resilience parallels the elasticity of memory. Remembrances arise when needed during everyday living. They support us when we need them.

Some days I feel the Presidio's *Spire* is the Mount Tsukuba Buddha in another form. I sit on the wooden slab bench and watch *Spire*'s charcoal splendor as it ascends into the stunning blue sky.

Sitting in *Spire*'s presence evokes the memory of once standing before a Buddha I met serendipitously on a mountain in Japan. I pilgrimaged through a forest I never would have found unless I rode a cable car resembling a yellow submarine up an unfamiliar mountain on a last-minute tour after a work assignment in Kyoto. When I think of this Buddha, I believe its spirit has guided me in stillness through the many years since we met. When I think of this Buddha, I smile.

FACT: My walk on Spirit Mountain, as I've come to call it, resulted from my daily meditative ambles during the pandemic. Just to breathe in the forest, listen to birds call to each other, and watch the coyote cross my path oblivious to my presence healed the isolation that I experienced during the pandemic's first years. I often hear travelers say, "I haven't processed the trip yet." It may take years for one's voyage to be understood fully. I learned to be present in each moment, to wonder at the great immensity of living handed to me at birth.

Forests

a Buddha crossed
my path once

and now abides
on Spirit Mountain

where I've come
to call home

Tagging vultures in the Ikh Nart Nature Reserve
in central Mongolia.

Mongolian Disco

Mongolia

I fully expected John Travolta to stomp out of the cold night air into the Sanitarium's disco ballroom. Vintage lights swirled around the room a la *Saturday Night Fever*. Wooden chairs lined the walls, circling the plank floor. The disco ball's multifaceted mirrors reflecting another time in American culture lit the faces of a cadre of Mongolians, five Americans, and two Japanese. We were ready to groove to the beat I hadn't heard in eons.

How did I end up in the middle of Mongolia, ready to boogie? A year earlier, I leaned into my bedroom dresser and stared at the photo of my grandmother and her adult children. Anna Bala Pramik gazed back. High cheekbones, her wry crooked smile inherited by my father, glinting eyes that knew something about going somewhere. She'd left Poland at age seventeen with her younger sister, landing on Ellis Island with five dollars in her pocket. Most young women in those times made the crossing with a husband to escort them across the Atlantic. Not Anna Bala.

Her open face staring at me said "Mongolian." The Tartars and Genghis Khan's hoards had crossed Poland at least three times during the 1200s. Unfortunately, Poland has no natural boundaries such as mountains, rocky cliffs, lakes, or rivers. If the Poles had any inkling of raids heading their way, they hid out in thick forests, plentiful on Poland's plains, and outwait the aggressors. Some of the Mongol armies' DNA may have blossomed in my grandmother's future genes after one of these forays. It's estimated that sixteen million men are genetically linked to Genghis Khan.

These musings and my scientific training spurred me to sign on to a citizen scientist tour to assist budding Mongolian researchers in collecting data at Ikh Nart Nature Reserve located five Jeep hours southeast of the capital, Ulaanbaatar. The COVID pandemic inspired me as well to live my "travel manifesto": travel with purpose, travel slowly, travel emphatically, travel with choice, and travel in joy. I wasn't after the tourist brag of horse races, falconry classes, *ger* sleeping, sheep herding—all those "authentic" Mongolian traveler experiences. I was after something deeper. My roots called, the reason I tread softly on this planet.

We began our two-week tour with no paved roads, just bouncing around on what may or may not have been the tracks of a previous Jeep.

Mongolians laugh at themselves a lot, said Gana, director of the nature reserve. She explained that Mongolians have many road songs about roads that go somewhere but are not really designated roads. Jeep tracks swirl all over the sandy surface of the Gobi.

"We have a song to Grandma's house. We have a song to 'Wedding Road' (about how to get to an individual wedding site). We have a song to find the sheep, the horses, the camels, the city, the town." She laughed. I looked out the side window. I saw the tire tracks of interloping four-wheel drives amid the vast expanse of the Gobi. Worn surfaces but few paved roads. Exquisite deep-blue sky flecked with fluffy cloud puffs met the rocky horizon. I believed my host when she said she hires the best drivers who know where they're going. All Jeeps come equipped with GPS while cell towers are rare in the area.

Gana Wingard, lead scientist for the Mongolia Research Program, set up a whiteboard in the dining *ger*. On it, she listed the names and titles of Mongolian researchers and staff, the five Americans in attendance, and the two Japanese teachers (who thankfully spoke some English). Born, raised, and educated in Mongolia, Gana also directs the affiliated program with the Denver Zoo Foundation. She spends about half of each year in Colorado.

"Select your *ger*," Gana instructed us as we tumbled out of the Jeeps and vans. A *ger* is the Mongolian cousin to the Turkish yurt, a few wooden poles strategically placed and covered by tightly layered felt. I moved my suitcase on wheels into the tent-like structure closest to the eco-toilet. By the end of my stay, I could speed to the eco-toilet in the darkest hour of night. The trek uphill to the two pleasantly clean, side-by-side rooms was two minutes one-way under the vibrant, crisp, and clear Milky Way. At night, the camp manager, Ulzii, kindly turned on the solar footlights along the path.

I'd dropped into the middle of active data collection for our team's project. No time for any discussion. Just go. We rose at the crack of the Mongolian dawn, six in the morning. I stepped out through the *ger*'s flap. A majestic ibex stood high on the cliffs above, keeping watch over the camp. Her two kids peeked out on the rocky bluff.

Gana runs a tight research ship. In August during my visit, Ikh Nart Nature Reserve research teams counted small rodents such as gerbils and field mice to determine if there was enough food for the fledgling and adult vultures nesting in the area. Remo, who broke out into a folk song at every opportunity, was our go-to senior researcher for these duties.

Next, quick vulture visit instructions: Check the data sheets for vulture chick capture and tagging, with many items to measure on the big birds. They weigh about 7.8 kilograms (17.2 pounds). Serchee is the vulture specialist, he had just received his Master of Science degree from the University of Mongolia.

A third, calmer project, or so I thought, involved counting and identifying the teeny plants in one square meter of Mongolian soil. Really? We all had to help count each species of plant in each coordinate of the nature reserve. Tuvshee was the resident vegetation expert. He was serious, spoke halting English (I could see his mind translating the perfect reply), and was a true academic. It was rumored he studied Mongolian flora well into the early morning hours. On the first day of counting, I struggled to sit on the ground while balancing the three-pound, multicolored volume titled *Flora and Vegetation of the Ikh Nart Nature Reserve*. I'd like to say this task got easier, but it didn't.

The second day, my teammates (Del and Gail, a husband-wife duo from Wisconsin; Karen soon to be living in Kentucky; Junya and Waka from Japan) and I were trained for one of the three data collection projects.

The third day, we all visited a vulture fledgling nest. As the oldest scientist, I tried to keep up using my hiking poles. They turned out to impede my progress, but I caught up eventually. I was a bit peeved at myself for aging. And slowing when I climbed boulders, huge boulders where vultures liked to nest. Of course, vultures would challenge us humans with huge boulders.

Serchee nimbly climbed up to the nest. He was twenty-something. He demonstrated placing the hood over the fledgling's head and embracing the young bird who would someday have a six-foot wingspan. He and his teammates measured and tagged the wing and foot of the chick who had not yet learned to fly. Serchee and his co-researchers' work over the past six years had discovered that these birds wintered in South Korea.

The foot tag had the email address of the Denver Zoo Foundation so that a bird spotter could inform Gana's team where the bird had been found. Each spring and summer, the grown fledgling fly back to Ikh Nart. They'd return home to the same area where they were hatched. To breed this time. No one needs to tell a vulture there's no place like home.

After a few days of this rigorous schedule, we'd jump up and hit the Jeeps before breakfast. Tseegii always had some snacks available—granola bars, oranges, and cookies (not my usual American diet) for our pockets and packs.

Later, Gana asked if I would like to interview the "locals": cook Tseegii, housekeeper Ariunaa, camp manager Ulzii, and Puugii, one of the drivers. These "locals," as Gana called them, were there because the camp was the only job around where they could earn hard cash. Earning money is especially difficult for the women in Mongolia. Honored, I agreed to these interviews. With Gana serving as translator, it was like talking to them directly. Secretly, I hoped to glean a closer understanding of my grandmother's Mongolian genetic tough grit.

The next day, we'd set aside several hours in the late morning after the breakfast dishes were dried and put away. The other Earthwatch volunteer teams had left at the usual eight o'clock hour. Tseegii, Ariunaa, Gana, and I huddled around the center table in the dining *ger*. The conversation was surreal. We talked, we laughed, and we joked as if we'd known each other all our lives. My eyes blurred. I asked reporter-like questions that most often veered into general discourse and hilarity. They felt like my Ohio cousins. The present moment seemed to cycle back to a time when family was family, and neighbors were friends.

The world had slowed; people were people everywhere. They treated me as a beloved guest, inviting me to get to know them. Sitting at the breakfast table that morning transported me to a memory of our family confabs around our picnic table in my Ohio backyard: gossip, trying to solve all the world's problems on a summer morning, and helping to resolve a family problem. I had much to ponder.

Ulzii, the camp guardian, lives year-round in his campsite *ger*. He was divorced with a 28-year-old son and two grandchildren who visited the camp at times. Among his twelve siblings, he has a sister who serves as the local veterinarian. We drove past her house, a concrete building standing out on the plain in stark contrast to the *gers* doting the landscape. According to Ulzii, the locals picked up newspapers in the town post office to keep up with the news. His many brothers and sisters came to visit. Inside his *ger*, I spied a television streaming at night. Apparently, Ulzii had connections. We passed many people on motorcycles or horses who all were noted to be Ulzii's cousins or uncles or brothers.

Tseegii was muscular with black hair pulled back in a bun; her deep dimples would make anyone smile because they formed a happy grin on her face.

"I want to be a truck driver," she revealed. She liked handling a big rig. Her natural strength would be put to good use. She was born in Ulaanbaatar, but her family originally hailed from just south of Ikh Nart. She finished eighth grade, then completed two years of vocational school in house building, designing metal-frame structures inside concrete. She was one of seven women in the class. Then she continued training in other fields, which led her to cooking at the camp the past four summers.

Tseegii met her husband in the same town. No longer married, she raised their two children, who are now young adults traveling the world. After that, Tseegii tended a guesthouse in Turkey. She also worked in a Mongolian store in China. Now she leads a seasonal itinerant life, taking jobs wherever she can earn cash.

Some of our translated conversations included presidential politics. And more laughter. Her daughter lives in South Korea, she said, and she planned to visit her later in the year. Tseegii's favorite work is driving cars and big trucks. The previous year, she drove a twelve-geared tractor-trailer in winter conditions, but it didn't meet her expectations. She likes dancing better, she explained.

"I know the name and face of each of my five hundred goats and sheep," said Ariunaa, age forty-four, who had worked at the camp for three years. How many sheep, goats, and horses a person has determines their worth in Mongolia.

Ariunaa's ten-year-old daughter tended the flock while her mother dusted out the sand and stones from our *gers* and kept the eco-toilet fresh and tidy, ensuring there was enough dried horse manure to cover the human waste. Again, the housekeeper job at Ikh Nart was a rarity—straight cash for three months of labor. Ariunaa's oldest son worked in a cement factory where he gravitated after vocational training in welding. The fluidity of Mongolian life choices amazed me. Without any judgment of her son, Ariunna spoke lovingly about each of her children. Her two younger boys still resided at home and attended school. "They have to listen to their dad while I'm away," she said.

Her plan: She'll work to support her children's college education. They'll board at the school during the week and visit home on the weekends.

Tseegii and Ariunaa then asked about my life in San Francisco. I explained that I worked full-time. Live alone. They were shocked that I had three children and had to keep working into my seventies.

"Which one of these children do you plan to live with when you get much older?" both asked, making me squirm at the intensity of their question.

Apparently, I hadn't thought this option through. I assumed I would not age.

The two women melted my heart. Looking me straight in the eye, they sincerely wanted to resolve my retirement dilemma. In Mongolia, the parent always lives with one of their children. Thus, Tseegii and Ariunaa reasoned, one of my children would have to step up to the task. I promised to discuss this with my three children on my return. They smiled, nodding approval. They seemed genuinely pleased to help me "resolve" this issue. A deep, abiding grateful warmth surrounded the table and filled the *ger*.

A few days later, the researchers and staff were abuzz with excitement. Disco night was upon us! Everyone had to attend. We had to dress in our best. I hadn't packed my dancing clothes as these were not on the what-to-pack list.

"During our high school years, we all learned ballroom dancing. We had to accomplish the four basic steps to graduate—waltz, foxtrot, polka, and tango," Gana said. Fear froze my body. I could not begin to distinguish among these four dances.

On the outer edges of Ikh Nart Nature Reserve flowed a healing mineral water spa. At the center of the spa, a disco ballroom was available to rent. Biyelgee traditional dancing still exists, but who knew Mongols loved ballroom and disco? Our nature reserve camp group of Jeep drivers, young scientists, a cook, and a housekeeper piled out of the four-wheel drive, ready to rock.

On this enchanted evening, Remo coaxed the ailing music machine to play assorted Mongolian ballads and folk songs. Though I didn't recognize the words, the beat moved my toes to tap and my body to sway.

Stayin' Alive played in my head. Then the disco player had finally kicked in.

No, John Travolta didn't prance onto the wood floor in a white suit.

But who knew Mongols loved ballroom and disco? Our camp group was ready to groove.

Gana cut an elegant figure on the dance floor. In a patterned long skirt draping her slim figure, she gracefully floated across the floor with every partner waiting their turn. A dapper older gentleman invited her to dance. A beautiful pair, he in his rakish fedora and front-tucked formal pants and long-sleeved shirt, and she, lithe and slim with long black hair flowing down her back.

The Ikh Nart group claimed the chairs along the walls. I guessed that Gana had instructed the drivers and young researchers to invite each of us foreigners to dance. No wallflowers allowed. They all kindly took their turns. The Mongolian crew were accomplished dancers and attempted to teach us their steps using minimal English. They mixed the pairings—women together, men together, men and women together—laughing and swirling. Each fellow guided me around the ballroom ignoring that I crunched their toes and tripped over my own two feet. Housekeeper Ariuuna took me aside and made a valiant effort to teach me the two-step. She could count in English. I counted too.

A young boy in a red shirt hung out of the refreshment window. Drinks were nonalcoholic: Coke and Fanta. Chips and strange-looking Mongolian delicacies spilled onto a shelf by the window. Flashing purple, fuchsia, and green light sliced over the ceiling, walls, and dancers.

Tseegii really rocked. I marveled at her lithe moves. Surely, she'd seen *Saturday Night Fever.* At least twice. Everyone knew how to enjoy the moment, throwing themselves into our two-hour camp break. They compelled me into letting go of some of my shyness, at least a little.

Stepping out on the veranda for cool air, I met a stylish Mongol woman. She said she lived in Paris year-round but came annually to the Sanitarium spa for the restorative waters. We invited her in.

The ride back to camp continued, joyous and raucous. It had taken over an hour to arrive at the disco but took only thirty minutes to return to camp. Grinning, our driver Jagaa sped over unmarked roads and bumped hills, taking shortcuts. A jerboa, the long-eared cousin of the gerbil, jumped into our headlights and led the way. I felt like Cinderella in her mice-drawn carriage heading home from the ball under the broad Milky Way.

Later, inside the *ger*, the pressed felt walls kept me warm, my thoughts close. I reflected on the spirit of these centuries-old nomadic people, open and friendly, laughing and supportive, in everything they did. I felt closer to understanding my grandmother through this journey. Her living in the now that I witnessed growing up in Ohio was so present in these individuals with whom I shared two weeks of my life.

FACT: The great expanse of the Gobi Desert and low population density leave Mongolia open to many effects of climate change. Its geographic location, extreme weather, and fragile ecosystems make the country's economy, livelihood, and traditional cultures vulnerable to climate crisis. Air pollution is a big problem in Mongolia's cities, especially in the capital, Ulaanbaatar. The country is warming at a rate three times faster than that seen anywhere else on the globe.

Sunrise

the Gobi Nature Reserve
    opens to the morning sky

Argali mother stands
high on the cliff
her kid peeks out
    to watch
        still sleeping
         campers

Polish delis sprung up on many streets in Dublin and other towns in Ireland after the influx of Eastern European immigrants.

Dancing the Irish Polka

Ireland

"We ♥ Polski" boasted the sign on the crusted red bricks of an anonymous storefront on O'Connell Street around the corner from Eden Quay and the River Liffey, one drizzly June morning in Dublin.

"Polish Spoken Here," glittered the only notice in another Dublin shop window on Parliament Street.

On my recent quest to Ireland to discover the modern Irish soul, I did not expect to find descendants of my Polish forbears populating the Emerald Isle. Apparently, newly affluent Ireland has become the prime destination of hard-working Poles unhappy about the slow-paced, still-in-transition Polish capitalism.

Steeped in Polish culture from birth in the eastern Ohio hamlet of Maynard, settled by Poles, Czechs, Slovenians, and a few random Italians, the proverbial Irish surprise slugged my psyche. Everywhere I walked, I encountered Poles flooding the streets of not only Dublin but all of Eire. In County Cork in the rebel southwest, many a native Corkonian lad has wedded many a Polish lass over the past decade.

Within the last fifteen years, the economy of the Celtic Tiger beckoned hundreds of international companies to set up operations. Low taxes and other fertile dispensations lured pharmaceutical and biotechnology companies, manufacturing and telecommunications industries. Close on the tail of this new prosperity, like dolphins and whales foraging after herring off the Irish coast, hundreds of thousands of immigrants set sail for the land of Erin. The Irish media reflects this change with new publications—three Polish (*Polska Gazeta, Sofa, Polski Express*), three African (*Eye, Bold and Beautiful, Xclusive*), two Lithuanian (*Lietuvis, Saloje*), two Chinese (*Shining Emerald, Tiao Wang Magazine*), and one each catering to the country's Russians (*Nasha Gazeta*), Latvians (*Sveiks*), Filipinos (*Filipino International*), and Pakistanis (*Pakistan Times*).

Most of Ireland's new "huddled masses" arrived from Eastern Europe countries. The majority, it seems, hailed from Poland. Polish workers are ubiquitous. Friend Joanna related that when she checked the internet in the Belfast public library, the Google default promptly appeared in Polish!

Poles. They are recognizable everywhere in Ireland: blond, with pale blue or deep brown eyes, fine features, a touching demeanor, and—I sensed—a sadness at being the "other."

"Are you Polish?" I asked.

Blond and upright in his well-fitted suit, the night clerk at Dublin's Trinity Capital Inn did not sound Irish. He answered my probe with a clipped certainty and an interesting, definitely non-Irish linguistic twist.

"Ya, sure," was his direct reply, much like my father's terse, no-nonsense retorts to my youthful queries. The young man explained that he was a computer engineering student taking time off from a Polish university.

"It's very difficult in Poland right now. The government is moving too slow in economic matters. Even a doctor cannot make an adequate income. Here, in Ireland, one can earn enough to live." He had spent the past year and a half working the nightshift at this Irish hotel directly across from Trinity College.

Poland, without any natural borders to protect its countryside and identity, harvests people who emigrate to survive, a characteristic they share with the Irish. All four of my grandparents left the green rolling hills of southwestern Poland for similar landscapes in Ohio and Pennsylvania at the dawn of the twentieth century. They bid farewell to mother, father, and siblings, like myriad Irish sailing to America from Cork harbor, never to see their loved ones again.

Today, many Poles in Ireland perform service sector jobs: shop girls sell Irish sausages, waitresses struggle with an Irish menu in a unique English accent, and au pairs in middle-class Irish homes nurture children for six to twelve months—work that the newly affluent Irish gladly hand off.

According to Witold Sobków, Polish Ambassador to Ireland, the Polish adore Ireland and revere it as a land of hospitality and beauty.

"The [Polish] people love Irish music, dancing,

Guinness, and whisky. We have Irish pubs in Poland; we celebrate St. Patrick's Day," said Ambassador Sobków in an interview. He also noted that Irish owners lease land to Polish farmers. Bicultural marriages occur each year, usually a Polish girl and an Irish boy plighting their troth.

It's estimated that some 250,000 to 400,000 Poles have relocated to the Emerald Isle, recently displacing Chinese as the largest minority. As with many courtships, the Irish-Polish relationship had a rocky beginning. On May 1, 2004, any person with a red European Union passport could traverse EU countries and work without a permit. Soon, newspaper articles and editorials ranted about how the Polish immigrants boosted crime. Next came claims of exploitation of Polish workers, and Irish groups assigned alcohol and drug abuse to this immigrant group. In 2006, members of a far-right neo-Nazi movement in Northern Ireland allegedly attacked Polish immigrants on the streets or in their homes. Graffiti in Derry shouted "Poles Out" underlined by a swastika.

"I know it's not my country, but it's my Europe... We will defend ourselves. We are not slaves," said Radoslaw Sawicki in an interview in 2005, when he organized Poles working for the Tesco supermarket chain warehouse in Dublin. The Irish trade union SIPTU supported him and his fellow Poles, who were making about two hundred euros less per week on average than their Irish counterparts.

These articles resonated with what I knew of the Polish immigrants who populated the Ohio River Valley. Coalminers, mechanics, and farmers, the Poles showed a strong affinity for unions, for solidarity, and for their religion.

Sister Eily Deasy, a recently retired teacher of the Sisters of St. Joseph of the Sacred Heart, visited us on our tour and described a young Polish woman named Ella who cared for her newborn niece. Sister Eily's sibling, Annette, recounted the devotion to the Church that Ella had shown, a trait inspiring trust from Annette and her family.

"We don't mind them usually, but they are lowering the wages here. They work for less than we would," said a tour bus driver in Cork City when asked about the influx of Polish workers. This is one opinion shared by several news stories. Much of the wage depression, though, emanates from unscrupulous Irish and Polish companies that prey on unsuspecting new arrivals, offering low wages and claiming them to be on par with those of Irish workers, an unfortunate behavior of corporations worldwide.

"I think the immigration is fine. We're getting used to it," opined the perky, red-haired proprietress of an Irish goods shop in the upscale tourist haven of Kinsale, County Cork.

"But I worry we'll lose who we are, what makes us Irish. You can go up through Ireland and not meet an Irish person in the restaurants and shops," she continued, straightening the hats and fabric bags on display.

At a Kinsale bookstore, a blonde twenty-something clerk with a pink chiffon scarf tied jauntily around her neck and seated at the register offered another view.

"I think the immigration is great. We like to have new people in. The Irish have had to endure so much criticism and prejudice over the years about themselves, I would hope we won't do that to others arriving here."

Ireland has traditionally dealt head-on with certain immigration issues. When some immigrant factions in England crossed the Irish Sea to birth their offspring in Ireland for citizenship, the government changed the law. They decreed that a person must live or work in the country two to three years before their child can become an Irish citizen at birth.

The Irish have always dealt with many of their challenges through music. Like the Irish, I turned to music for answers as well. Like a bee to pollen, I moved toward it. I could hear an accordion a mile away. On any recording, my ear tunes into the melodious chords from every squeezebox. My mother, in her sainted wisdom, proclaimed there would be at least one musician in our family, and that would be me. I learned to play a proper Polish polka at age five.

One night at the Armada Pub in Kinsale, County Cork, Sean Pol and accordion joined a group of four other musicians. In the daylight hours, he said he labored as a validation engineer two miles down the road at Eli Lilly. With an infectious smile and his instrument strapped to his chest, he smoked Irish jigs on his American-made Hohner harmonica. The rhythm and tone sent me back to the ritual Saturday nights of Polish weddings at home and the all-day Sunday polka party on our black 1950s radio.

As the four musicians cranked out the flings and jigs, I could see Frankie Fudale and sons Billy and Jimmy and their orchestra busting out polkas and mazurkas as the townspeople back in Maynard, Ohio, danced well into the Sabbath. Whisky and beer flowed freely.

The Irish pub scene, with professional and amateur musicians wandering in or invited in, also brought back scenes of many a family party with cousins brandishing their instruments and Uncle Joe huffing on his harmonica. I was always commanded to break out the black-and-ivory accordion to play those darn polkas, including "Mila Baba Koguta" ("A Lady Had a Rooster"), my mother's favorite.

In addition to a love for lively music, Poles share the Roman Catholic religion with the Irish. While some resurgence in paganism and spirituality imbues the island, Ireland remains a Catholic country. With younger generations stoked by the Celtic Tiger's money-first focus, international travel, and connection with same-aged populations on other continents, the Catholic Church's influence has waned. Yet the 2006 Irish Census found that 3.68 million Irish of the country's 4.6 million inhabitants check the Catholic box for religion.

The Catholic Church in Ireland now has new supporters. Away from home, Poles continue their fervent attendance and devotion to the mass. At St. Augustine's Catholic Church in Cork City, long lines of Polish young men wend around the pews as each waits his turn for the confessional on a Saturday evening. Father Pat Moran, pastor at St. Augustine's for thirty-seven years, is elated by the energy contributed by the Polish congregants. The weekly Polish mass runs for ninety minutes, drawing some Irish locals among capacity crowds. Some Irish parishioners view the Poles as echoing the Irish in the Sixties when they dispersed throughout the world like so many dandelion seeds because of the economic condition at home.

Michael O'Brien, our regular taxi driver in Crosshaven, County Cork, spoke strongly on the topic of Polish immigration.

"I'm happy about it," he said. As well he should be since he married Marianne, who crossed over from Poland ten years earlier. Michael said he hired Marianne for a job at his taxi company employer. And the rest is history.

"She cooks Polish food for me and some Irish dishes as well," said Michael proudly. Michael and Marianne O'Brien had recently become new parents, and their bonny lass, six-month-old Michelle, was named after her papa.

"When I came to Crosshaven two years ago, only six Poles lived here. Today there are more than one hundred Polish," said Magda, the dark-eyed energetic waitress at The Anchorage Pub in Crosshaven. Magda had followed her accountant husband to Ireland, bringing their two young sons, aged three-and-a-half and two years.

"In Poland, the minimum wage is two hundred euros a month. Here in Ireland, I can make two hundred euros for three days of work at this pub," explained Magda with a bright smile. In Crosshaven, her family finds it easy to blend in, noting that they have Irish, French, Spanish, and German friends.

"I work here as a break from my sons," Magda cheerily confessed, turning her energy to delivering the best bowl of seafood chowder of our Ireland stay. Later, she noted that forty years of communism had created much infighting and distrust of the government in Poland so that many there "half-hate, half-love" Poland. She said she planned to enroll her boys in an Irish school, stay ten years, and then see what would happen back home.

Ireland has surprised itself, it seems. The new influx of immigrants resonates with so many Irish. For generations, they left their island in search of work. Not always welcome in foreign lands, today's Irish try to do one better.

During my stay, O'Brien Press announced they were translating the popular guide *How the Irish Live* into...Polish, of course. The radio news announcer said: "This is a new group sharing our island with us, and let's give them the traditional Irish welcome: *Céad Míle Fáilte*, One Million Welcomes."

The Irish have some lessons for us all on immigration and graciousness. Their openness of spirit provides a glimpse into the modern Irish soul. Indeed, 'tis much like the Irish soul of old, so much so that it makes a person feel like stomping and twirling. Ah yes, strike up that Irish polka, and let's all dance!

FACT: Poles migrated to Ireland about twenty years ago largely because Ireland allowed immediate entry to its labor market after Poland was admitted to the European Union. As citizens of the European Economic Area, Poles had the right to migrate, live, study, or work in Ireland, where they receive social security and healthcare. As the climate crisis produces more and more rapid environmental havoc, human migrations will increase, blending cultures and transferring internal allegiances.

Nomads All

sorrow
leaving home
never again
to gather lilacs
growing
on grandmother's
south lawn

migration
polishes people
    shines them
    as if stone

The above-ground graveyards in Greece allow family visiting.

My Greek Ancestors

Greece

I am the only Greek in my family. The fishing net draped across the front entry adds a definitive new leitmotif to my San Francisco Edwardian home. The building has a blue-tinged white luster much like the structures that cling to the angular precipices of Greece's southern Peloponnese area of Lakonia. According to Greek lore, the fishing net, having survived the washings of forty different currents, is so pure and clear that it will bless my home and guard against evil. You see, I've just returned from Greece and have discovered my true Greek ancestry.

The charm against the Mati, the Evil Eye, now dangles on my rearview mirror as I speed along California's highways. The Greeks believe this talisman protects a person from another's bad vibes or harmful thoughts. I have obliged each of my daughters to wear the deep blue "evil-eye" amulet and have secretly pinned one inside my son's drumstick bag as well. He will attend music school in New York City soon, and goodness knows he'll need it there.

My family's genealogy records show that each of my four grandparents emigrated from Poland to America's port of entry, Ellis Island, where their names are clearly chiseled on the stainless steel panels on the island's perimeter. Cousins have produced a photographed copy of Grandpa Pramik's signature on the entry legend when Poland was occupied by Austria. However, I have often suspected that I was adopted. The childhood fable, "The Ugly Duckling," had a deep resonance for me during my tender years.

My sojourn in the Peloponnese clarified how growing up in a Polish, Czech, and Italian hamlet in Ohio prepared me for Greek life. Cabbage rolls look a lot like dolmades. My mother made great summer salads. She chopped cucumbers and onions, adding oil and vinegar for the vegetables to swim in. Virginia (Vir-gee-NEE-ah to her Greek compatriots), our host for the Vatika workshop, mirrored my mother in her cooking. Greek dishes flowed from her tiny stove. The kitchen, compact and complete, resembled the galley of a ship, taut with stored white café dinnerware and authentic antique pottery. I searched everywhere with my eyes but could not see where she stowed food supplies that would appear on her table for the next meal. My mother cooked like this, always prepping twice as much food as was needed. Just in case. In case more people appeared at the door, such as the family member who brought the other cousins who just happened to be in town. The Polish tradition of setting a place at the table for those family members who had died had taught me to always set an extra place.

Here, as we faced Neapolis Bay and the Aegean Sea beyond, a staple of nearly every meal is the Greek salad. Not the usurper we have in the United States but the veritable Greek horiatiki salad composed of luscious vine-picked tomatoes, slivers of Vatika's sweetest red onions, slices of cucumber, and black Kalamata olives—and delivered with a thick slice of the whitest succulent feta dusted with Mediterranean spices and drizzled with olive oil. Finally, a blessing of lemon juice is sprinkled over the riotous mound of colorful vegetables.

Noodles were another part of my upbringing. Haluski, a blend of flat pasta, cabbage, butter, and onions sautéed to perfection, readied me for Virginie's noodles and cheese casseroles. My grandmother baked cheese pies with a touch of sweetness while Virginia, our Greek mother for the week, crafted cheese pies that hosted a savory tanginess and zest I hope to soon emulate in my San Francisco kitchen. One evening, at a wine tasting featuring local Vatika wines, we were treated to a meat platter that featured sliced sausage, much like the Polish kielbasa, and keftedakia, akin to meatballs. However, liquid refreshments on the southern peninsula varied from Polish thirst quenchers. In Vatika, we were treated to excellent deep red *krasi* (wine) from the Monemvasia region rather than the traditional Eastern Europe whisky shot with a beer chaser.

In Virginie's kitchen and at her table, I ate without stopping, those second helpings tasting even better than the first. All of the Greek dishes laden with vegetables whispered "wholesome," "natural," and "light" because they were made with the secret ingredient of love.

Virginia always set the table with a Grecian blue tablecloth. Breakfast included thick Greek yogurt squeezed to a consistency of pudding and laced with honey from the countryside and jams reminiscent of the berry jams of my childhood. The same blue cloth hosted lunches of the obligatory Greek salad and basket of sliced bread; cheese pie (*tiropita*) with its flaky filo; noodles and cheese; and aubergine with a filling of hard cheese baked with tomatoes and herbs. Some days a fish dish would appear. Other meals were vegetarian fare that overwhelmed the palate and sated the soul as well as the body. I had no problem adapting to this diet.

In Greece, mothering is a part of the psyche as well. Gracious, attractive, svelte, stylish, able to wear a white sarong in a multitude of knots and ties, Virginia quite magically prepared dinner and "light" lunches that carried us through the afternoon, all the while serenading us with Greek folk songs of love and Piaf-esque ballads and minding her children in Athens. Virginia, kissing all on one cheek and then on the other, was our earth mother, the all-accepting mother I had always wished I had.

Hugs and *filakia* (kisses) are the Greek greetings among men and women. For those of us caught in the sanitized computer age, this ritual can take a bit of getting used to. Kissing both cheeks and hugging as a greeting was performed by all. Several times our taxi driver would hop out and joyously greet a neighbor while we waited and watched. I had always longed for that human touch. American life can feel empty with its "ships passing in the night" existence. I knew I was Greek because these boisterous greetings and energetic kisses felt so natural.

I have always used my hands when speaking. My own mother once asked if I was Mediterranean, focusing on the Italian love for hand gestures. She should know, I thought, when I was old enough to question authority (age five). Her query was my first inkling that I was different, an ugly Mediterranean duckling floating in the wrong Ohio pond.

Then last year, I met *agapi mou* (my love) Connie, one of our hosts for this summer's Greek revelry, on a journey in France. Her hand pirouettes quadrupled mine. I had found a kindred spirit! One who bestowed a welcome on both cheeks while speaking volumes with her hands.

In Greece, I could use my hands without embarrassment. Like the wide flapping of a swan, I need not shy away from flamboyant circles. Watching Connie diagram the air, messages arced across the atmosphere, her fingers declared, "I'll see you at four o'clock precisely." Taxi drivers, when not crossing themselves, would drive with their left arm dangling out the window and wave minute textual greetings to fellow drivers or pedestrians in passing. The palm facing inward with a "come here" motion means a goodbye among Greeks. An outward-facing palm with five fingers splayed was not a good idea, though, as the inhabitants consider this a rude gesture. No wonder taxis did not stop for the five American goddesses using standard NewYorkese for "Taxi, please."

Another inherited Greek trait, Greek Maybe Time, or GMT, operates as a genuine center of my biological clock. My children can attest to this evidence of my Greek ancestry. They often grew impatient with my "I'll be right there" responses to their pleas for attention, which would take hours on certain days. Now I realize that the abundance of unfinished projects decorating my home parrot the multitudinous unfinished houses that mark the Greek landscape. Hulks of rebar and dark gray concrete, shrines to GMT, heartened my views. Rather than dampen the vistas, they spoke to me: "Ah, life is so full, with so little time to do everything."

After spending nearly two weeks in Greece in the hillside village of Mesochori on the southernmost point in the Peloponnese, I was certain of my Greek roots. Little do my children realize that I have begun their dowries. Greek parents buy each daughter a house upon marriage; I may have to bend a little on this one as my son would feel slighted. Although a law canceled the dowry or *prika* in 1983, parents still bestow refrigerators and beds, and sometimes houses, on their female offspring. With today's California housing prices, I may have to attenuate this long-held custom. Perhaps I could buy each child one of the myriad unfinished homes that languish in the villages of Lakonia, next to hotels, or across vacant lots in Athens, adjacent to glorious classical buildings.

Upon my return from the Peloponnese, I prepared meals resembling Virginia's. Greek spices infused my cook's psyche. California vine-ripened tomatoes and crunchy cucumbers in season in mid-July created a real Greek salad. As I served my brother a Sunday meal in my newly inspired Greek goddess persona, he quipped, "How long is this Greek phase going to last?" He'll rue the day he made that comment. He is the only blue-eyed member of our Ohio Polish family. My son, however, seemed taken with the baklava and chunks of sweet melon swimming in native juices served with every dinner. My slicing and arranging the red and light-green fruit on the plate seemed to bless the flavors a hundredfold, just as Virginia's hands did in Mesochori.

Henry Miller in *The Colossus of Maroussi* observed, "For a Greek, every event, no matter how stale, is always unique. He is always doing the same thing for the first time...." Living in Greece for nearly two weeks set my Greek DNA vibrating.

Dancing on Connie's patio in Neapoli on a balmy July evening awaiting the full moon brought back a flood of memories of customary Polish weddings celebrated nearly every weekend in my Ohio hamlet.

Connie's American-born nieces counted out the steps to the traditional *hasapikos*: one-two, cross over, three and four, five, six, seven, eight. The intensity of the nieces' tutelage and the preciseness of the count could not counter the effect of the magical essence of the local wines. Inhaling the night, I stopped counting the steps after several dances and gave in to my inner Greek. "Just sway with the music," my genetic memory counseled. *Opah!* Ah, then my steps flowed. My hips swayed under the white tulle skirt, and the night air picked up my steps. Around we twirled, circled. I caught sight of Orion's Belt in the dark sky. I had begun to glide like a graceful swan across the stone floor, no longer awkward or foreign.

Living among these welcoming people, I experienced *parea*, the Greek word for belonging to the human community. A swan among the swans, let's say. Today's Greeks welcome all into their community. It's a palpable, intensely real emotion.

Although Ellis Island registers my grandparents as Polish, perhaps they honeymooned in Greece a century ago. In the past, ancestors were known to have traveled far and wide. After two weeks among the oregano and thyme and the incessant cicadas and promising figs, I am convinced that I am Greek. My heart tells me so.

FACT: On my first trip to Greece, living in southern Neapoli, I enjoyed dancing in the full Zorba-the-Greek way. I so wanted my AncestryDNA test to confirm my Greek lineage. It didn't, of course. To tourists, Greece is a welcoming country. Greeks spread their arms to boat survivors even when their country is wracked with debt imposed by world financial systems. The Greek welcoming heart remains open to migrants reaching for its shores.

Welcome

some countries
have a heart

some countries
    break hearts
    with their beauty

Greece opens its
    beauty to those
    seeking a home

St. Mary's Church in the Karków Central Square. Every hour on the hour, a trumpeter (from firefighter volunteers) emerges from the uppermost left tower window and plays the *Heynal*.

Matriarch

Poland

The voice of passion is better than the voice of reason.
The passionless cannot change history.

—Czesław Miłosz

As a child, I always felt more Polish than American. Growing up in eastern Ohio amid the relentless rural poverty of a coal mining town, my five-year-old fingers banged out raucous polkas and mazurkas on the child-sized used accordion my mother scraped enough together to buy. She seemed to think that all Polish children had a genetic predisposition for the accordion, and I didn't prove her wrong. The bellows smelled of cigarette smoke and whisky, but the sounds from the squeezebox sparkled. My most treasured possession, I often caressed its "diamond"-encrusted button marking the middle C on the left chord panel.

I delighted my sister and three brothers (who often

sat with tiny fingers in their ears just to annoy me), dozens of cousins, assorted aunts and uncles, and fellow parishioners with "Miala Baba Koguta" ("A Lady Had a Rooster") and "Piwo Piwo Czerwone" ("The Red Red Beer"). I dreamed of playing in a polka band in "the Old Country," as Grandma Anna Bala called it. I would impress Polish citizens across the land in a homecoming tour from Gdansk to Warsaw, turning south to Kraków. I spent many a snowy evening poring over the map of Poland in our burgundy *American Peoples Encyclopedia*, plotting my route.

Every Sunday after mass at St. Stanislaus Church (Poland's patron saint), we'd seek out the welcome smells of sweet fresh-baked sweet breads and *golumpki*, the infamous cabbage rolls that filled Grandma Anna's kitchen. From a primitive wrought-iron stove, she'd prepare exquisitely tender cinnamon buns, breads, and pies—rhubarb was her specialty. Our church-going families feasted on roasted chicken and other dishes laid out on the oilcloth-covered table. After cleaning up, the Polish chatter would begin. I didn't speak Polish really. But I intuitively understood what and who they spoke about. Every so often, a sprinkling of an English word lit up the air. I was a sleuth in search of meaning.

I'd sit snuggled on the third step of the narrow stairway to the upper rooms while my cousins played outdoors. I stayed glued to my seat, entranced by the village gossip entwined with the family's political arguments. I pieced together a history. I heard much talk of "resistance," among other things I didn't understand. I heard whispers that an uncle who returned with shell-shock after World War II may have later committed suicide. The Poles had both contributed to the monstrous crimes against the Jews and Romany and fought against those abominations. The Polish resistance lost many heroes, shot down in town squares. Warsaw was flattened; only two churches remained standing at armistice.

Though my family spoke only Polish at these gatherings, I easily followed their stories. We all spoke Polish then, or so it seemed to my child self.

In 2008, after my father's funeral, my childhood friend Eddie Goletz presented me with an exquisitely folded United States flag from the Maynard American Legion Post in Belmont County, Ohio.

"You are now the matriarch of the Pramik family," Eddie said as he laid the flag in my outstretched hands.

As the eldest of five, I was not so sure my siblings were happy to hear this pronouncement. Growing up, my parents often tasked me with minding the younger ones, and I took my job seriously, with little humor. Many arguments resulted from my exactitude; sticks were swung, dirt thrown, tomatoes splattered new shirts and dresses, windows broken. Now, I had to assume a different mantle.

Eddie's declaration opened my eyes to what I had to do.

What are the duties of a matriarch?

First, I looked to the matriarchal achievements of other animals, specifically elephants and orca whales, both known for their strong, long-lived matriarchs. In *Beyond Words: What Animals Think and Feel*, conservationist Carl Safina writes about the matriarchal behaviors of those two animal groups. Safina cites the elephant cows, who lead herds to water, safety, and community well into their nineties, and discusses studies of aging female orcas in the Pacific Northwest finding food for their pod and communicating with humans.

I then researched human communities: the Mosuo of China thriving in the Himalayan foothills; the Minangkabau (Minang) of Indonesia; the Bribri from Costa Rica and northern Panama; and the Tuareg, the nomadic Berber people of the Sahara. I learned that a matriarch needs no one's permission to carry out her duties (perfect for me). She doesn't necessarily have to make decisions or "rule" a family; she is valued for her mere presence. This matriarch's life sounded better every minute. She was not a witch or a hag. She didn't have to be a mother, though many matriarchs have children. She possessed the inner knowledge of herself and what she does best. Full of self-confidence, the matriarch transitions into a rich life full of conscious awareness, intuition, enjoying the moment, and celebrating others' accomplishments. The matriarch knows she does not have all the answers, but she excels at listening and encouraging others to believe in their own choices. I liked this job description.

A matriarch cannot resolve anyone's pain, according to another source, but she can ease it with her comforting presence. She reminds others that, though they struggle, they are loved. They would always have a place in her home or walk beside her. Now the matriarch of the Pramik clan, I began to understand this underlying responsibility to extend a calm welcome to family, friends, and the world as community. I began to understand this duty to perform, to understand this purpose bequeathed to me for the next forty years or more of living.

My grandmother, Anna Bala, left Poland in 1899 with five dollars in her pocket, based on the records of her arrival on Ellis Island. She also had her year-younger sister in tow. And she was unmarried when she crossed the Atlantic, quite uncommon in those days. Upon learning that she had traveled so far with so little into the unknown, I felt the genetic pull for my underlying wanderlust.

I had to wait to ease my feeling of *fernweh*. A German term, it's sometimes defined as "far-sickness" for a home one has never visited. I could see the flowers, the window shutters, the cows, and the chickens in my great-grandmother's garden. The worldwide Depression and overwhelming responsibilities of raising a large family begat a dogged, heads-down approach to living. Everyone followed the planting seasons. Digging potatoes and other root vegetables and storing the bushel baskets in the hillside cellar overtook their lives, as did the harvesting and canning of all foods. They had experienced severe hunger. The world seemed to expand, blow up. Family members lost touch with each other.

None of my grandparents ever returned to Poland. The Depression, two world wars, and extreme poverty prevented them from even considering the possibility of traveling home.

Grandma Anna had two younger sisters born in Poland who she never met. The Atlantic Ocean created a rift in the family tree that proved irreconcilable for decades. Then there was the matter of the Russian domination of Poland during the Cold War. An array of restrictions complicated traveling to Communist Poland. My own pilgrimage to my grandparents' birthplace had to wait more than sixty years while I traveled like an American to the *de rigueur* tourist cities of London, Paris, Rome, Amsterdam, Mexico City, and Istanbul before finally setting foot on Polish soil.

After the overthrow of the Communist government in 1989 (and the departure of the Russians in 1993), my father's youngest brother, my Uncle John— a lawyer, FBI agent, and CIA consultant who spoke fluent Polish and Russian—decided to find our remaining relatives in Poland. He traced Grandma Anna's Polish home to the southern town of Rokiçiny, between the Tatras Mountains and Kraków. He did this almost exclusively by word of mouth.

After one assignment in Moscow, he and my Aunt Caroline returned to Rokiçiny, where he chanced upon a roadwork crew. He asked if anyone knew where the Pramik family lived. One worker stood up.

"I'm a Pramik," he said.

From my grandmother's stories, my Uncle John had tracked down her sisters. He located her two nieces, the daughters of her youngest sister. They corresponded over the years until Uncle John died.

My childhood family rarely went on a vacation. A Sunday ride through the Ohio countryside became a major event of our summer months. As a single parent in California, I understood the economy of staying home. I too plodded on, raising three children from middle school through college. Working full-time to pay the education expenses alone took all my energy and effort. Travel was the ultimate luxury.

After my youngest child graduated from a music conservatory in New York, I opened a savings account optimistically labeled "Travel." After squirreling away funds for more than five years, I joined my wealthier siblings, a Pennsylvania brother and sister, on an ancestral odyssey.

My suitcase clattered over the cobblestones of Kraków. My niece Aniela, then living in this World Heritage city, and I wandered through the main market square, called Lesser Poland, which dates to the thirteenth century. The Nazis had spared Kraków. Without bombed rubble, the UNESCO World Heritage Centre felt genuine. The clock struck two in the afternoon, and the window of the St. Mary's Church tower opened. A trumpet emerged from the tower window with a young man playing the *hejnal* save for the last note.

In the electric afternoon sun, I shivered, reliving my favorite grade-school book, Eric P. Kelly's *The Trumpeter of Kraków*. I stared up at the sunlit figure leaning out of the tower. I imagined the nobleman's family fleeing the Tartars from what is Ukraine today). The sire shouts at his wife, children, and servants: "I must establish the night trumpeter in St. Mary's Church. Only for a short time. Go hide!"

The nobleman tasks the trumpeter to play the *Heynal* song every hour. This song honors the first young trumpeter who warned the townspeople of the impending invasion in 1215. A Tartar arrow pierced the first trumpeter's throat, stopping the last note. My throat knotted up, and tears sprang just like the first time I read the book. In the face of danger, the boy, near my age, fulfilled his duty to his town. Kraków today honors the tradition of this song, each hour on the hour, twenty-four/seven. It continues today, played by Kraków's firefighters. That day, I watched and listened to a young first responder extend his trumpet through the narrow window of the tower and play the *Heynal*... without the final note. The ache of the note's absence clung to the air.

Our guide Piotr arrived the day after I did in a minivan. In his mid-thirties with black-framed glasses and dark hair, he energetically assured us of his expertise in ancestor hunting. He worked through a Polish ancestry service out of Chicago.

We piled into the van, headed for Zakopane in the Tatras Mountains. First, we'd stop in the town of Rokiçiny, where Uncle John had reported finding Pramiks and Balas.

"I called the parish priest at the church in Rokiçiny and asked to see the parish records," said Piotr. "He said we could look at them at four o'clock on Friday, on our return. I'm not sure why he specified this time."

We planned to leave Kraków on Wednesday morning. We'd have a long wait ahead and then only an hour to check the parish ledgers on Friday's return. I began to feel a bit glum about any family discoveries on this trip. So did my siblings.

What we didn't know was that Piotr was indeed a practiced genealogy sleuth. We drove through lush green countryside speckled with small towns and villages that resembled the rolling Ohio hills where we had grown up, and my brother Joe gave voice to my thoughts.

"I can't believe how much this place looks like Maynard!" The poplars, maples, and locust trees, the zinnias and peony bushes, cried out *home* to each of us.

We drove into Rokiçiny at one in the afternoon. Because the priest had set Friday for our visit, I assumed it would be a drive-through this time around. Piotr had other plans. He sped around the hills on narrow roads, past a schoolhouse, and then backed up to ask a farmer on a tractor, "Where's the parish church?" (I'm only guessing because his Polish was far too fast for my ears.) He told us he'd also asked about the location of the Pramik compound from other locals several times. I wondered how we could locate anyone's home because of the lack of street signs in this village of 1,450 inhabitants.

We found the new church atop one of the town mounds, and next to it, the rectory. We parked in the gravel lot below. It was Wednesday, now one-thirty in the afternoon.

"Come, we can see if the priest is home." Piotr hustled up the hill. Schooled in reserved American manners, we hesitated. When we caught up to Piotr, he'd already bounded onto the rectory porch and pounded on the polished-wood entry. Several moments passed, and then the priest—in black T-shirt, black pants, and tussled hair—opened the door. I suspected he'd been napping.

Piotr presented our dilemma. The scheduled time of Friday at four would be quite late to start a search for cousins amid these hills. However, we *did* have time now on our drive to Zakopane. We would not disturb the priest. He could go about his parish work, and we could peruse the registry out here on the porch if need be. (At least I imagine this is what Piotr said with so much passion and speed that the priest, holding his gold-rimmed spectacles in his hands, looked puzzled.)

Piotr told the priest the Pramik name and the year our grandparents emigrated. We followed the reverend into his office, slightly bare with papers strewn on a desk. He pulled down two large black leather ledgers and opened one; Piotr looked over the priest's shoulder and immediately noted that it was "too recent." They chatted about dates of birth, or so it seemed. The priest then left the office, to return with yet another very worn, fading black ledger. Together, he and Piotr scanned the pages.

"This is the one!" said Piotr, visibly excited. He asked if we could photograph the birth records. With exquisite precision, Piotr's fingers and eyes scanned the elegant script in each column.

"Here are all the Pramiks: five sons and three daughters. Jan Kontin was the eldest son. Your grand-father is written down here too—Augustin!"

"We knew him as August Pramik," I murmured. We were incredulous. So easy, so fast. A miracle, if I believed in miracles.

I snapped photo after photo as fast as I could, feeling like a spy. When we finished, it was three-thirty.

We thanked the priest, bowing to his presence. He spoke no English. I'm sure Piotr made the proper thanks. He asked the priest if he knew where the Pramiks lived. Standing out on the porch, he waved over toward the hills and murmured something about a railroad crossing, or so Piotr informed us.

We jumped in the van and sped (as fast as one can on single-lane rutted roads) toward the center of town. Piotr veered off to the left.

"This might be the road. See the tracks? I don't know if trains come here now." An incredible July green coated the hills. We turned into another single-lane road that led past an old barn and a mud-and-wattle structure. Beyond lay several more modern homes.

"You see this hut? This is where your grandfather may have been born. These are the original buildings here." Piotr steered the van over potholes and steep turns, bouncing his cargo. He clearly loved his work.

We pulled past one house and then rounded a corner to the right into a makeshift driveway. Nothing would stop Piotr now! He knew he was closing in. Springing out of the van, Piotr made a beeline for the front gate, and we scrambled after him to the wooden porch. Rapping loudly on the door, his sunglasses in his hands, he stood expectant, smiling.

An older woman opened the door, smiling. Piotr blurted out who we were.

I was aghast. No way would we do this in the U.S.! We could be shot for banging on someone's door unannounced, especially in coal-mining country.

The woman, her dark hair silvered with gray neatly arranged in a bun, smiled wider.

"I remember Augustin! He always sent us clothes and money in the really bad times. I think this skirt I'm wearing came from him," Piotr translated.

This woman was Zofia, the eighty-year-old wife of our eighty-seven-year-old second cousin, Augustin, who sat ailing inside the house. She fit into the beige tweed flecked skirt after more than half a century.

My niece Aniela spoke her excellent Polish to Zofia. After some chatter, she said Piotr had asked if we could visit on our return from Zakopane on Friday. Of course, Zofia's face showed her excitement and pleasure about the upcoming visit. She would have Augustin ready and would inform his eighty-two-year-old brother Stanislaus, who lived in our grandfather's house around the corner, of our visit. We made plans to stop again on our return from Zakopane.

"This really looks like Ohio," commented brother Joe.

This would become our mantra during the remainder of the journey. The house, the flowers, and the concrete walk to the porch all mirrored our parents' home in Ohio. I snapped photos of the rainbow of flowers and shrubbery. Golden marigolds, pink-red roses, lavender, fuchsia asters with pale white centers, all planted in arrangements similar to my mother's flowerbeds.

In under three hours—and after fifty years—we'd found our living family in Rokiçiny, where they had resided all this time.

The two days spent in Zakopane zipped by. The Friday visit loomed in our collective mind; we seemed to discuss it several times a day during our tourist wanderings. We shopped for handmade chocolates and a bouquet of mixed blooms for Zofia and Agustin.

When we arrived in Rokiçiny on Friday, the couple was dressed and ready to greet us. Zofia wore a navy two-piece outfit, and Augustin sat composed and polished on the sofa.

"I had to give him his heart pills, he got so excited about your visit," Piotr and Aniela translated. Zofia gazed fondly at her husband of more than fifty years as Augustin sat with hands folded in his lap, a beatific smile on his weather-worn face. Augustin had worked on the railroad his entire working life. Zofia brought over a photograph of her handsome young husband when she first met him. "Quite a good-looking fellow," she murmured, beaming at the color photograph.

We stood at the window, looking out on the Pramik compound. It included five hectares of land surrounding the house and up the back hill. The couple lived with their granddaughter, who taught English in a nearby town and was working on the day of our visit. "She takes care of us and will inherit the Pramik land," said Zofia, who offered us simple cookies.

Stanislaus arrived, all vigor and bustle. At eighty-two, he'd survived four heart attacks yet spoke with vitality and passion. A bachelor all his life, he still lived in the original house of his parents, where my grandfather was also born. He'd worked as a plumber and farmer on this same parcel of earth.

As he orated and Piotr and Aniela translated, I was transported into a zone of fluid understanding. The same zone as when I sat in Grandma Anna's kitchen after Sunday mass. I'd known this man all my life. He spoke in Polish, but I knew what he said. He spoke of the horrors of the war, the ghastliness of the death camps. I was suspended in time. His stories sounded like my grandmother's stories, my mother's stories. I felt the yarns intertwine with the double helices of my cells.

"But the Russians were brutal, worse than Nazis. They pitted family members against each other. If they wanted your cow, they took it because they said the State shared in the property." Stanislaus's blood pressure visibly rose remembering Communist times. The Russians did not permit them to learn English during those days.

Stanislaus stopped and then hurried to his house, bringing back his father's passport from 1927. His father, Jan Kontin, had traveled to the United States several times but always returned to Rokiçiny. Jan led his family's polka band in town, said Stanislaus. They were a musical family, with constant dancing in the house.

Aha! My mother was correct about the accordion in my genes, in my fingers. Polkas run in the family—more DNA dust.

Stanislaus then gave us a grand tour of his three-room home, the house in which my grandfather Augustin was born. Modest, clean, organized. Paintings of Jesus and Mary hung on the walls. A church calendar was centered on one of the kitchen walls. Again, just like my mother's kitchen in Ohio.

Next, Zofia invited us to pay homage to the family's burial site. She would show us Jan Kontin's grave and the Pramik plot in the new cemetery. We loaded into the van with Zofia sitting in front, directing Piotr.

"The graveyard just grows and grows, and now it's flowing down the hill," Zofia joked. She'd brought a votive candle and matches. We followed her along the narrow paths between the close-set gravestones and monuments. At Jan Kontin's resting place, Zofia lit the candle, signed herself, and prayed for the head of the Pramik clan. Wholly welcomed into Zofia's life here on a sunny September afternoon, I was in awe. No pretense, no awkwardness. Of course, she knew we would want to visit the eldest Pramik brother's grave. An old country family ritual to follow, I scribbled this in my rapidly filling matriarch notebook.

Piotr asked Zofia if she knew where the Bala

family's home stood. Yes, she thought could find it. She waved her hand over several hills to the south. Again, as co-pilot, Zofia directed Piotr to the Bala house. One building connected with the other; three houses and a barn linked across the compound. *This is where my Grandma Anna was born.*

Hurdling through a flowered trellis, Piotr addressed the five people standing in the yard. Was this the Bala home?

Yes, it was.

We met Genevieve and Maria, daughters of Anna Bala's youngest sister, Ludvica, whom she'd never met. Maria's thirty-something son stood nearby. He understood and spoke English. They had had two brothers, Edward and Stanislaus, both now deceased. Their father had worked in America for seven years but returned to Rokiçiny. Genevieve, about seventy and wearing her hair pulled back in a bun, was the very image of Grandma Anna Bala. Both women remembered Uncle John and Aunt Carolyn's visit. They loved the letters he wrote in Polish.

"But the letters stopped a few years ago," said Maria. Yes, they'd stopped: Uncle John had died four years before our visit.

"On your next trip you can help us dig potatoes. Then we will have a barbecue," Walislav, Maria's husband, joked in surprisingly fluid English.

We exchanged photos and hugs and addresses. Another whirlwind gathering of a clan I'd just met. The red zinnias and orange marigolds, the oilcloth table covering, the swaying poplars again resembled our Ohio neighborhood.

At the Pramik compound, Stanislav pointed to a small tractor standing in the yard that they had built. It was made of metal and rubber pieces fashioned like a Rube Goldberg claptrap machine. Stanislav said they wasted nothing. The tractor looked like something my father would have crafted at my childhood home. My father never bought something new just for the sake of owning a new contraption. He invented solutions, making the most of whatever he had on hand.

It was early evening. I watched an extremely old woman, bent over at a forty-five-degree angle, walking gingerly with a staff up the long green hill next to Zofia and Augustin's home.

"That woman is ninety-five years old," said Stanislaus. "She's walking to dig potatoes."

I watched, making a mental mark in my matriarch journal.

I still had to earn the title. I needed to practice, much more.

The perseverance and resilience of family live over the centuries and cycle through my veins. In every cell. Like the trumpeter's call from Kraków's St. Mary's Basilica every hour since the thirteenth century, Poles embrace a heritage of resilient solidarity.

Watching the *staruszka* climb the hill that evening, I connected with people who shared my tribe's code.

These traits continue deep within me. Eldest sibling, caretaker, explorer, welcoming spirit. My current tasks require that I wear the mantle of matriarch, mother, giver of light and life over the earth each day as I participate in living this world's history.

FACT: Poland experiences the climate crisis much like the United States: environmental stresses, extreme weather, unexpected heavy rainfall, wildfires, and deteriorating water quality. Polish authorities believe climate change is the biggest threat mankind has faced in the last decades. The security situation continues to be volatile as well. As part of my role in resolving the climate crisis, I pledge to care for the planet, leaving the smallest carbon footprint when visiting other countries.

Motherland

petals strewn on paths
   marigolds, asters, petunias
  same flowers
     different countries

peonies grow
by the front porch
     caring for the home
     as rains fall

Call to Action: Do Something

Pray to God, but row away from the rocks.
—Hunter S. Thompson

Pray to God, but don't stop swimming to the shore.
—Russian saying

God is good, but don't dance on a small boat.
—Irish proverb

In short, *do* something. Even taking small actions can ease our hopelessness and fear while reducing the impact of the climate calamity that's bearing down on us. Whether we're buying carbon futures, attending protests, disinvesting in fossil fuel companies, investing in reforestation, writing letters, or simply always washing our clothes in cold water, we *can* help. Crucially, we need to lead the way for our children and grandchildren, who will battle problems that have been ignored for decades, such as the warming oceans and sea-level rise, in the years to come. The time is now to address this crisis. The storm clouds are upon us.

Publication Notes

Pilgrimage to the Ice Continent

"Pilgrimage to the Ice Continent" won a Silver Award in the 2022 Solas Awards for Best Travel Story of the Year.

A version of this essay, "Antarctic Pilgrimage" has been published at https://medium.com/@mjpramik/soul-on-ice-7915f009eab

Winds of Mesochori

"The Winds of Mesochori" won a Silver certificate for the Solas Awards for Best Travel Story of the Year in 2020.

"The Winds of Mesochori" was published in *Venturing in Southern Greece. The Vatika Odysseys.* ©2006.

The Drummer's Heart

"The Drummer's Heart" won a Silver Award in the 2013 Solas Awards for Best Travel Story of the Year. "The Drummer's Heart" was published in *Venturing in Ireland.*

Quest for the Modern Celtic Soul. Palo Alto, CA: Travelers' Tales. ©2007.

Running in Puglia

"Running in Puglia" won a Silver Award in the 2010 Solas Awards for Best Travel Story of the Year.

"Running in Puglia" was published in *Venturing in Italy. Travels in Puglia, Land Between Two Seas.* Palo Alto, CA: Travelers' Tales. ©2008.

Peaceable Kingdom

"Peaceable Kingdom" was published in *Wandering in Costa Rica. Landscapes Lost and Found.* Oakland, CA: Wanderland Writers. ©2010.

Paradise Lost and Found

"Paradise Lost and Found" was published in *Wandering in Bali. A Tropical Paradise Discovered.* Oakland, CA: Wanderland Writers. ©2012.

Eighth Wonder of the World

"Eighth Wonder of the World" has been published at https://medium.com/@mjpramik/eighth-wonder-of-the-world-108d1daf6653

An Open Door

A version of "An Open Door" appeared in *Clips & Pics. Bay Area Travel Writers and Photographers*. United States. ©2014.

Coal: Black to Gray and Back (Down in the Mine)

A version of this essay, "Down in the Mine," won a Silver Award in the 2023 Solas Awards for Best Travel Story of the Year.

"Gray to Black" received an Honorable Mention in the 2016 Solas Awards for Best Travel Story of the Year.

"Black to Gray and Back" was published in *Wandering in Cornwall. Mystery, Mirth and Transformation in the Land of Ancient Celts*. Oakland, CA: Wanderland Writers. ©2015.

A version of this essay, "Down in the Mine," was published at https://medium.com/@mjpramik/down-in-the-mine-black-to-gray-and-back-c5b81c859518

Ghost Ship: USS Hornet Conducts Spook Maneuvers

"Ghost Ship" won a Silver Award in the Solas Travel Awards in 2016.

Nun for a Day: Wandering in Koyasan

"Nun for a Day: Wandering in Koyasan" was published in *Wandering in Japan. The Spirit of Tokyo, Kyoto and Beyond*. Oakland, CA: Wanderland Writers. ©2022.

"Nun for a Day" received an Honorable Mention in the 2019 Solas Awards for Best Travel Story of the Year.

Parahawking in Nepal

"Parahawking in Nepal" was selected by Bradt Travel Guides for publication in *To Oldly Go. Tales of Intrepid Travel by the Over-60s*. Guilford, CT: The Globe Pequot Press Inc. ©2015.

"Parahawking in Nepal" won a Bronze Award in the 2016 Solas Awards for Best Travel Story of the Year.

A version of this story, "Grounded: Learning to Fly Solo," won a Silver Award in the 2020 Solas Awards for Best Travel Story of the Year.

A version of this story, "When There's No Time Left for Fear," was published in *Deep Travel. Souvenirs from the Inner Journey*. Jacksonville, OR: Deep Travel LLC. ©2019.

An Evening at Café Clock

"An Evening at Café Clock" was published at https://medium.com/@mjpramik/an-evening-at-cafe-clock-d1f05aa3001.

Know Thyself: The Octopus and Me

A version of this essay, "Food for Thought," won a Silver Award in the 2023 Solas Awards for Best Travel Story of the Year.

A version of this essay, "What I Learned from the Octopus," won a Bronze Award in the 2022 Solas Awards for Best Travel Story of the Year.

A version of this essay, "Know Thyself," won an Honorable Mention Award in the 2021 Solas Awards for Best Travel Story of the Year.

"Know Thyself: The Octopus and Me," was published in *Wandering in Greece. Athens, Islands and Antiquities.* Oakland, CA: Wanderland Writers. ©2020.

"Know Thyself: The Octopus and Me" was published at https://medium.com/@mjpramik/4ccef1441be6

Mongolian Disco

"Mongolian Disco" won a Silver Award in the 2022 Solas Awards for Best Travel Story of the Year.

Dancing the Irish Polka

"Dancing the Irish Polka" was published in *Venturing in Ireland. Quest for the Modern Celtic Soul.* Palo Alto, CA: Travelers' Tales. ©2007.

My Greek Ancestors

"My Greek Ancestors" was published in *ODYSSEY* magazine. May/June 2007.

Recommended Reading

The following list of books, arranged alphabetically by author, is curated based on my voracious readings on the climate crisis, climate change, and climate chaos over the past decade. Some of these volumes point to the immensity and diversity of our amazing earth. However, some of the most stunning thoughts on where our planet is headed during this climate crisis are contributed by novelists, fiction writers, and poets, who often lead the way in understanding the immediacy of the *now*.

Susan Alcorn. *Healing Miles: Gifts from the Caminos Norte and Primitivo*. Oakland, CA: Shepherd Canyon Books. ©2017.

James Bridle. *Ways of Being: Animals, Plants, Machines: The Search for a Planetary Intelligence*. New York, NY: Farrar, Straus and Giroux. ©2022.

Douglas Brinkley. *Silent Spring Revolution: John F. Kennedy, Rachel Carson, Lyndon Johnson, Richard Nixon, and the Great Environmental Awakening*. New York, NY: HarperCollins Publishers. ©2022.

Stephen Harrod Buhner. *Plant Intelligence and the Imaginal Realm: Into the Dreaming of Earth*. Rochester, VT: Bear & Company. ©2014.

Rachel Carson. *Silent Spring*. New York, NY: Houghton Mifflin. ©1962.

Pema Chödrön. *When Things Fall Apart: Heart Advice for Difficult Times* (20th Anniversary Edition). Boulder, CO: Shambhala Press. ©2016.

Danny Dorling. *Slowdown. The End of the Great Acceleration—and Why It's Good for the Planet, the Economy, and Our Lives*. New Haven, CT: Yale University Press. ©2020.

Paul Douglas. *A Kid's Guide to Saving the Planet: It's Not Hopeless and We're Not Helpless*. Minneapolis, MN: Beaming Books. ©2022.

Jonathan Safran Foer. *Eating Animals*. New York, NY: Little, Brown and Company. ©2009.

John Freeman (Editor). *Tales of Two Planets: Stories of Climate Change and Inequality in a Divided World*. New York, NY: Penguin. ©2020.
Seth Godin. *The Carbon Almanac. It's Not Too Late*. New York: Portfolio Penguin. ©2022.

Temple Grandin. *Visual Thinking*. New York, NY: Riverhead Books, Penguin Publishing Group. ©2022.

Nicos Hadjicostis. *Destination Earth: A New Philosophy of Travel by a World-Traveler.* London and New York: Bamboo Leaf Press. ©2019.

Thich Nhat Hanh. *Love Letter to the Earth*. Berkeley, CA: Parallax Press. ©2013.

Thich Nhat Hanh. *Zen and the Art of Saving the Planet*. New York, NY: HarperCollins Publishers. ©2021.

Paul Hawken. *Regeneration. Ending the Climate Crisis in One Generation.* New York: Penguin Books. ©2021. *An enormous list of tasks each of us can choose from...to do something!*

Katharine Hayhoe. *Saving Us: A Climate Scientist's Case for Hope and Healing in a Divided World.* New York, NY: Atria/One Signal Publishers. ©2021.

David Hinton. *Wild Mind, Wild Earth. Our Place in the Sixth Extinction.* Boulder, CO: Shambhala Publications. ©2022.

Elizabeth Kolbert. *Under a White Sky: The Nature of the Future.* New York: NY: Random House. ©2021.

Elizabeth Kolbert. *The Sixth Extinction*. New York, NY: Henry Holt and Company. ©2014.

George Marshall. *Don't Even Think About It: Why Our Brains Are Wired to Ignore Climate Change*. New York, NY: Bloomsbury Publishing. ©2014.

Peter Matthiessen. *The Tree Where Man Was Born*. New York, NY: Penguin Books. ©1972.

Charlotte McConaghy. *Migrations* (novel). New York, NY: Flatiron Books. ©2020.

Orrin H. Pilkey and Keith C. Pilkey. *Global Climate Change: A Primer*. Durham, NC: Duke University Press. ©2011.

Richard Powers. *The Overstory* (novel). New York, NY: W. W. Norton & Company, ©2018.

Kim Stanley Robinson. *Ministry for the Future* (novel). London: Orbit Books. ©2021.

Carl Safina. *Beyond Words: What Elephants and Whales Think and Feel* (A Young Readers Adaptation). New York, NY: Roaring Brook Press. ©2019.

Eva Saulitis. *Into Great Silence: A Memoir of Discovery and Loss among Vanishing Orcas.* Boston, MA: Beacon Press. ©2013.

Susan Simard. *Finding the Mother Tree: Discovering the Wisdom of the Forest.* New York, NY: Knopf. ©2021.

Rebecca Solnit (Editor), Thelma Young Lutunatabua (Editor). *Not Too Late: Changing the Climate Story from Despair to Possibility.* Chicago, IL: Haymarket Books. ©2023.

Rebecca Solnit. *Wanderlust: A History of Walking.* New York, NY: Viking. ©2000.

Maya K. van Rossum. *The Green Amendment. The People's Fight for a Clean, Safe, and Healthy Environment.* New York: Disruption Books. ©2022.

David Wallace-Wells, *The Uninhabitable Earth. Life After Warming.* New York, NY: Penguin Random House. ©2019.

Acknowledgments

I have so many people to thank for making my pilgrimage on this planet exciting, interesting, and joyful: My three children—Danika, Madeleine, and Joe—who raised me through their childhood. And my grandchildren, Henry and Charlotte, who inspire me to preserve this planet for them. A special thank you to Madeleine and Joe for their contributions to the critical review of the text and poetry appearing in this book. And immense thanks to Joe for his enthusiastic work on the cover design. Gratitude to Ketzia Jacoby for her commitment to all creatures great and small and for sharing her love for good pure food.

Gratitude by the buckets to:

Madeleine who believed in this book, reading the renditions of these essays over many years. David Pramik, my brother, who patiently answered my photography questions by the thousands, even when they were repetitive, and who lovingly and meticulously produced most of the photographs in this book.

Lisa Segal, special teacher and poet, who can see meaning when I cannot.

Jack Grapes who has taught me to look for my voice and not stop writing until I find it, and who taught me that I have a place in the world.

Travel gurus/guides: Don George, Tim Cahill, Larry Habegger, Jeff Greenwald, Phil Cousineau, Christina Ammon (travel writer, mentor), Erin Byrne (who pushed for the spirit in writing), Sivani Babu and Sabine Bergman, Linda Watanabe McFerrin and Joanna Biggar (teachers and editors extraordinaire). Laurie McAndish King and Jim Shubin for their generosity and enthusiasm for writing and publishing.

Janis Cooke Newman, esteemed meditation and writing teacher, who taught me how to breathe.

Travel buddies, friends, and extraordinary editors Donna Hemmila and Gayle McGill.

Bob Cooper for editing and proofing the current manuscript.

And to so many more friends with whom I shared these journeys over the past decades.

Sister Mary Carmella, my exceptional high school teacher, who inspired my love of science and Shakespeare at the same time.

Poets and spiritual guides: Federico García de Lorca, Constantine Cavafy (ah, Ithaca), Thanasis Maskaleris, Thich Nhat Hahn, Brenda Hillman, Robert Haas, Jane Hirschfield, Victoria Chang, Ada Limón.

Shirly Fernando, luminous and generous guide, who brought Sri Lanka alive and sparkling and sparked a friendship deeply felt.

Zakia Elyoubi, courageous storyteller from Fes, Morocco who follows her heart.

Graciela de Lara, who made our friendship of fifty years a welcoming reason to travel, especially to Mexico.

The Lit Splinter regulars Carole Stivers, Ida Hart, Jacqueline Hampton, Gail Ansel, Lita Kurth, Cindi Badiey, Cathey Daniels, Emily Cooke, Ria Talken, and Miryam Bujanda, among others, whose weekly Zoom presence kept my writing life alive during the isolation of the pandemic and continues to inspire me into the present.

About the Author

MJ (Mary Jean) Pramik began her travels on the fateful morning when her mother sent her alone to buy a quart of milk at Moxie's store in the hamlet of Maynard, Ohio. She gripped the dollar bill in her fist and navigated the gravel and dirt road to the blacktop where a red brick building housed the town's bodega. She returned home triumphant; she'd completed her first solo journey at five years of age. Inspired, she began walking and traveling.

MJ Pramik has spent more than thirty years as a professional science, medical, and technical writer for major universities and biotechnology companies. She holds a graduate degree in biological sciences, worked as a bench scientist at the University of California San Francisco, completed a Master of Fine Arts in Writing from the University of San Francisco, and taught graduate writing skills at San Francisco State University. She has coauthored peer-reviewed research papers, regulatory documents, and marketing campaigns. Her articles and essays have appeared in *Nature Biotechnology* and *Medical World Tribune* as well as *Good*

Housekeeping and the *National Enquirer*. She also penned the scientific thriller, *Norenthindrone, The First Three Decades,* the fast-paced history of the first birth control pill extracted from a Mexican yam.

Currently, she is completing her novel, *GEM of Egypt*, a family saga of immigration, the Depression, and the United Mine Workers Union in Ohio.

Follow her travel and science adventures and publications at her website: https://www.mjpramik.com.